# Dignity of Work

## Theological and Interdisciplinary Perspectives

Edited by
Kenneth Mtata

on behalf of
The Lutheran World Federation—A Communion of Churches

Lutheran University Press
Minneapolis, Minnesota

**Dignity of Work–**
**Theological and Interdisciplinary Perspectives**
**Documentation No. 56, December 2011**

Kenneth Mtata, editor
on behalf of The Lutheran World Federation – A Communion of Churches

Translation: Office for Communication Services
Editorial assistance:  Department for Theology and Ecumenical Relations
Layout: Department for Theology and Ecumenical Relations
Design: LWF-OCS
Cover: © Lutheran World Service India Trust

Published by Lutheran University Press under the auspices of:
The Lutheran World Federation
150, rte de Ferney, PO Box 2100
CH-1211 Geneva 2, Switzerland

Parallel edition in German available from Kreuz Verlag, Stuttgart, Germany

Library of Congress Cataloging-in-Publication Data

Dignity of work : theological and interdisciplinary perspectives / edited by Kenneth Mtata.
    pages cm
    "On behalf of The Lutheran World Federation-a communion of churches."
    Parallel edition in German available from Kreuz Verlag, Stuttgart, Germany.
    ISBN-13: 978-1-932688-68-9 (alk. paper)
    ISBN-10: 1-932688-68-4 (alk. paper)
    1.  Work--Religious aspects--Christianity. 2.  Labor--Religious aspects--Christianity. 3.
Christianity--Social aspects.  I. Mtata, Kenneth, editor of compilation. II. Lutheran World
Federation.
    BL65.W67D55 2012
    261.8'5--dc23
                                        2011048179

Lutheran University Press, PO Box 390759, Minneapolis, MN 55439
Manufactured in the United States of America

# Contents

# Foreword

## Martin Junge

This volume in the LWF Documentation series grew out of the symposium on the theology of work held on 2 May 2011, at the Ecumenical Center, Geneva, Switzerland. The seminar was organized by the Department of Theology and Studies of the Lutheran World Federation (LWF) and included participants from all LWF units as well as other ecumenical organizations, the International Labor Organisation (ILO), a local pastors' fraternity, faith-based community workers and scholars from the Ecumenical Institute at Bossey, Switzerland. Organized in recognition of International Labor Day, the aim was to kick-start an annual reflection on the notion of work from the perspective of faith.

Work or labor constitutes a fundamental aspect of human existence regardless of whether or not one believes in God. Individuals of all cultures and traditions associate work not only with sustenance but also identity. While work provides us with the means to afford shelter, food and clothes, human beings find deep satisfaction when their work and creativity are recognized by others. We feel useful when we create and produce things with our hands or as a result of our ideas. Work is one of humanity's qualities that was not completely lost after the fall. Rather, human beings continued to identify with their work.

Nonetheless, the conditions under which people work have often been far from dignified such as for instance the abomination of slavery. While for many slavery is a phenomenon of the past, today, as industries strive for the highest profit possible, production has shifted to those countries where wages are low and the rights of workers not respected. Child labor is a reality in many countries, where children are obliged to leave school in order to contribute to the family income. Other work related injustices include the trafficking of children who are forced to serve as begging slaves or to work in dangerous environments as child soldiers.

The Lutheran heritage regarding work as a vocation is most insightful in our effort to understand the meaning of work in our time. As vocation, work becomes an opportunity for human beings not only to participate in God's continuing work, but also to preserve creation, God's own work. In other words, in work we are invited to join God. This invitation should result in what God saw when God had finished creating the world and saw that "All was good." It is my hope that our communion of churches will seek this goodness as we reflect on work also in our local contexts.

# Introduction

## Kenneth Mtata

Work is one significant area of contact between faith and the world and as such an important topic not only for faith communities. Work does more than merely provide us with the means to meet our basic needs. Work can enhance the quality of life, making our lives more enjoyable. Human satisfaction is not only derived from what we produce as a result of our work; work also affirms our worth as human beings.

In the Christian tradition, creation, redemption and sanctification are God's work. These provide not only the theological paradigm on work, but can also provide inspiration regarding how we think about and carry out work. Creation—the work of God—is characterized with "goodness" as was manifested when God looked at the final stages of each creation: "And God saw that it was good" (Gen 1:10).

The more hostile aspect of work is encountered in the redemption, which resembles humanity's work after the fall. Work became painful and alienating. As depicted in the Gospel of John, Jesus came to earth to do his father's work: "My Father is working until now, and I am working" (Jn 5:17), or "We must work the works of him who sent me while it is day; night is coming, when no one can work" (Jn 9:4). Thus, redemption is in continuity with the work of creation. Work is however seen as more that merely creating or producing and provides more than material satisfaction: "Do not labor for the food that perishes, but for the food that endures to eternal life, which the Son of Man will give to you…" (Jn 6:27).

God's presence through the spirit in every form of creation sets apart all of creation. Engaging with creation therefore means that all spheres of noble work are sanctified.

The way in which perspectives on God's work can impact our own understanding of work has also been discussed in the area of economic ethics. The German sociologist and political economist Max Weber (1864–1920), for instance, concluded that religious or theological inclination influences work ethics. While this subject is not specifically dealt with in the essays included in this publication, it is hoped that Weber's conclusions are put to the test, confirmed and challenged by the reflections on the theology of work contained in this volume.

Drawing on the Old Testament, Kathryn Johnson's brief sermon introduces the topic of work and Christoph vom Brocke's and Andreas Kunz-Lübcke's contributions focus on the Old and New Testaments' understandings of work respectively. The creation story is central to the Old Testament introduction to our subject. Changes in perspectives can be observed as we move from the creation story to the story of the fall up to the collective work of building a city in Genesis 11. The New Testament perspectives on work can be understood at the intersection of the Jewish and Greco-Roman contexts. While not promoted in the former, hard or manual work and slavery are closely connected in the Greco-Roman milieu of the New Testament. Another important factor informing the New Testament theology of work is the eschatological hope as suggested by the injunction, "Anyone unwilling to work should not eat…" (2 Thess 3:10ff.).

Tom Kleffmann gives a broad overview of Martin Luther's theology of work as the basis for a just economy. One major thrust of Luther's theological reflections on work—the notion of vocation— is the understanding that faith discloses the broader meaning of work. Here human beings are liberated to grasp the divine sense of work through faith in the experience and knowledge of the justified life— justification and just relationships become closely connected in this sense. Kenneth Mtata and Martin Robra focus on how work is understood in two very different contexts: traditional Africa and industrial Germany. The significant change in the perception of work in the African context is the result of the encounter with colonialism, missionaries and other internal factors. In Germany, the economic slump prior to World War II, the decline of heavy industry and the outsourcing of production jobs have led to the loss of jobs in Europe. This has raised new challenges for both the workers and the local churches, attended by both employers and employees. Pierre Martinot-Lagarde suggests that the politics of work and the work place ought to be of great interest to the church for the obvious reason that the church's membership comprises both employees and employers.

Referring to her work among migrant workers in Geneva, Switzerland, Roswitha Golder observes how skewed against women the world of work is. Using the example of Swiss bankers' salaries, Edward Dommen points out that ethical considerations are not taken into account when huge salaries are negotiated for a few executives, while the rest of the workers are left scrounging for the leftovers. Veikko Munyika emphasizes that the human body—the most important tool—should be considered seriously when reflecting theologically on work. In the context of HIV and AIDS such a discussion has become critical. Roger Schmidt provides insightful, concluding remarks on how work and the understanding thereof have evolved over the centuries in the Western world.

Work is central to the shared life within and outside the communion of faith. Work can be both an experience of affirmation or of alienation. What we produce can enhance or destroy life. The fruits of our labor can be shared equally or become the basis for greed and marginalization. It is our aim to continue providing a platform for further theological reflection on the many facets of work.

# God's Work and Ours
## A Meditation at the Beginning of a Symposium on the Theology of Work (Gen 2:2-3)

### Kathryn L. Johnson

Our service today follows a different sort of liturgical calendar: it has been planned in honor of one of the Labor Days, International Workers' Day, which we celebrate this year not on May 1 but, because of our day of rest yesterday, May 2. It is in honor of this day that the Lutheran World Federation (LWF) invites you to attend a symposium on the theology of work. For this day, I will begin by reading a different sort of text, a poem about work and about ourselves by the contemporary American poet Marge Piercy:

> The people I love the best
> jump into work head first
> without dallying in the shallows
> and swim off with sure strokes almost out of sight.
> They seem to become natives of that element,
> the black sleek heads of seals bouncing like half-submerged balls.
>
> I love people who harness themselves, as ox to a heavy cart,
> who pull like water buffalo, with massive patience,
> who strain in the mud and the muck to move things forward
> who do what has to be done, again and again.
>
> I want to be with people who submerge
> in the task, who go into the fields to harvest
> and work in a row and pass the bags along,
> who are not parlor generals and field deserters
> but move in a common rhythm
> when the food must come in or the fire be put out.
>
> The work of the world is common as mud.
> Botched, it smears the hands, crumbles to dust.
> But the thing worth doing well done

has a shape that satisfies, clean and evident.
Greek amphoras for wine or oil,
Hopi vases that held corn, are put in museums
but you know they were made to be used.
The pitcher cries for water to carry
and a person for work that is real.[1]

I suspect that, in such a house as this, the affirmations of that poem ring true for most of us about our experience of work—even on a lovely Monday morning, when perhaps jumping headfirst into work like a sleek seal into water requires a bit more effort than usual. Now I ask that you think with me in relation to our biblical readings this morning about its closing affirmation: "The pitcher cries for water to carry, and a person for work that is real."

Perhaps our sermon text for this morning from Genesis 2 surprised you a bit as a text to think about work—for it is not in any obvious way a reading about us and our tasks. What we heard was about God: God rested from "all the work" of creation by taking a day off, it seems—and then by "blessing" and "hallowing" this day of rest. In these short verses, we are poised between what most of us here have been taught to call the first and second creation accounts in Genesis. We still have in our mind's ears the ringing rhythmic phrases in chapter 1 that describe the six days of creation—powerful, poetic, "liturgical" language that evokes worship for the immeasurable power of God's Word, the uncontainable movement of God's spirit. This is a God, who in the imagery of our own time "spins the whirling planets." And we know that just after our text come the vivid, down-to-earth verbs describing God's intimate closeness to creation—God forms the human figure from dust, breathes into nostrils, plants a garden, and walks among its trees. This is a real hands-on, hands-dirty sort of God. Our short reading this morning, coming between these two passages, provides us with a sort of breathing space at the top of the universe, and we can pause for a moment to rest, to catch our breath, before we go down again to where God and human beings walk together among the streams and trees of the garden.

But what an amazing pause this is. This is the first time the verb "work" appears in the canon of our Scripture, and its subject is God. God worked and worked well, creating what is good and very good and then also resting and blessing and hallowing the rest which follows after work. From the perspective of the biblical canon, whatever is said afterwards about people and their work is said only after it is said that God works, and then rests from that work—rests like laborers we know but in mysterious ways before them.

---

[1] Marge Piercy, "To Be of Use," in Garrison Keillor (ed.), *Good Poems* (New York: Penguin Books, 2003), 157–58.

Then, having spoken first about God and the divine work of creation, the Scriptures can draw truly remarkable consequences from this beginning. Human life is to be a life of work—not in the way of external command or sentence to hard labor but as this activity flows from God's own life. Genesis tells us, we recall, that humanity was created "in the image of God"—and the phrase, twice repeated in Genesis 1:27, is then left tantalizingly unexplained. I want us to consider that, coming so soon after the language of "God's image," the references to God doing good work in creating are perhaps part of the meaning of human life as *imago Dei*.

But this is also the first time we hear the verb to rest. And, so, if working is an aspect of life in the image of God, then so is the succession of working and rest which we find in our verses from Genesis this morning. We have not always focused first on this rhythmic dynamic life of work and rest as an aspect of the divine image. Perhaps this is in part because when we come to these first chapters of the Bible we have so often focused on what these creation narratives have to say to our questions concerning gender relations and sexuality. Not unimportant topics, to be sure—important not only for us, as we realize, but also for the communities of faith who shaped and first listened to these texts.

Some recent interpreters have alerted us that these communities have also had burning interests in the questions of work. Think about how the Scriptures continue: from this reference to God's good work and holy rest, we come at once in the second chapter of Genesis to the garden, where human involvement in gardening and caring for animals and bearing and raising children are all hinted at in the most ideal terms. But by the time we leave this garden the conditions for all these God imaging works have been changed by human disobedience, and the work that is to come afterward is hard, sweaty and painful toil—much more like what we recognize from the world as we know it.

Imagine how these stories of how work became a burdensome toil could sound to a people whose crystallizing community memory was the story of slavery and then the Exodus, release from bondage. What is slavery but endless toil: the capture, the theft of work; the grinding down of the fulfillment of completing one's tasks to nothing but an unceasing round of futility; the suppression of the rhythms of work and rest which allow joy and creativity to restore themselves after exhaustion; the denial that the slave, with the master, has a place equally in the divine scheme of work and rest?

What if we read these stories of God's creating work through the lens of the memory of God's liberating work in bringing Israel out of slavery?

Then, if we look to Israel's laws, we will see that the injunctions to keep the seventh day as a time of respite from work point in two directions, just as our verses from Genesis hinge together two different sorts of story. The laws of the Sabbath point on the one hand toward God, whose holy day it is. It is a time for worship, for conscious attention to the relation to God. This is the aspect which Martin Luther's *Small Catechism*, for example, especially picks up. On the other, Sabbath laws hold before us those most vulnerable to the abuse of their labor—those who know work most oppressively as toil, the sort of hard, grinding slog which requires respite. Thus the weekly day of rest comes as commandment—especially so that those with most control over working conditions cannot deny the day of rest to others. Keep the Sabbath, the Holy One commands, "so that your male and female slave may rest as well as you" (Deut 5:14). And indeed the rest extends past the household to all the population of Israel, including the migrants, and even the animals who shared in the human toil: "Six days you shall do your work, but on the seventh day you shall rest, so that your ox and your donkey may have relief, and your homeborn slave and the resident alien may be refreshed" (Ex 23:12). The Sabbath is both an ideal rhythm of life for Israel because it is an imaging of the life of God, as well as an honoring of God's work by sharing also in God's rest. And it is also a law for Israel because it is the recognition that human work is exercised in trying and far from ideal conditions that require restraint, balance and care for the whole ecology of relationships which binds together laborers of all sorts, animals and even land.

Our Ruth text this morning, which was chosen because it points us to the topics for the morning's symposium, gives us a vivid snapshot of the realities of work. In this account of the work of harvest, we see a community which provides a place for the less powerful to survive at the corners and edges of the work of the more prosperous. In allowing Ruth to gather part of the crop from his field, Boaz and his household honored the protections of the law, which also include Sabbath rest. But these arrangements do not of course return the field of Boaz to the garden of Eden; they underscore the special vulnerability of the outsider and the widow even as they provide some protection for it.

But these reflections take us further than we can go in this worship. It is time for us to go to work. So let us conclude by returning to the verses we read from Psalm 90. The day which begins with a prayer to "satisfy us in the morning with your steadfast love" comes to express a fervent prayer that God's work may be manifest to us, God's servants, precisely in the prospering of the work of our hands. Even in the difficult circumstances of waiting and longing which the psalmist describes, even in the full consciousness that our mortal lives wither quickly like the grass, still we ask God to fulfill the work of our hands. "The pitcher cries for water to carry, and a person for work that is real."

On this Labor Day, may our work be real work. May it work together with God's work for the fulfillment of the callings of all who bear God's image, and for the flourishing of all that God has made.

# Human Work from the Perspective of Creation Theology

## Andreas Kunz-Lübcke

The biblical prehistory account in Genesis 1–11 speaks principally of the world created by God and of human beings as God's creatures, evoking many aspects of human existence: the relationship between man and woman and sexuality in particular, interpersonal conflicts and the (disrupted) relationship between humanity and God. The subject of work is a common thread, cross-cutting all these themes and demonstrating how work is an integral aspect of human existence within the framework of creation theology.

## Creation and Shabbat—liberation from work

The two creation accounts at the beginning of the Old Testament (Gen 1:1–2:4a and Gen 2:4b–3:24) deal with the subject of work in two very different ways. The first creation account, which is generally considered to have been written during the exilic period, does not say anything explicit about the subject of human work. People are granted dominion over nature: over fish, birds and the beasts of the earth (Gen 1:26). This was to be done in a way described by the Hebrew words *kavash* and *radah*. While *kavash* implies the forceful conquest of a land or the subjugation of a people, *radah* generally refers to responsible royal sovereignty. Just as a king is responsible for the welfare of his subjects, people may not just abuse and exploit the animals under their control. Numerous interpretations of this passage assert that it refers to animal husbandry; in depicting humanity as the masters over the animals and over the land, it paints a static picture of human work.

The last part of the text clearly turns to the subject of work:

> And on the seventh day, God finished the work that he had done, and he rested on the seventh day from all the work that he had done (Gen 2:2).

God's rest is expressed using the Hebrew word *vayishbot*. This is a clear allusion to Shabbat, the seventh day of the week, on which people are obligated to cease all work. The first creation account, however, seeks to express much more than just an anticipatory justification for the later Shabbat commandment—that God personally rests from God's work after six days, pausing from God's action as Creator, must also be understood as a requirement. Work, growth and increase cannot be limitless. The requisite day of rest from human work imposes a pause on the human drive for profit and securing one's existence.

## Work and hardship: a history of alienation

The second creation account addresses work in a completely different way. Human life before the fall is not conditioned by freedom from work.

> The Lord God took the man and put him in the garden of Eden to till it and keep it (Gen 2:15).

Before the fall, people were not left to live lives as mere idlers into whose mouths "roasted pigeons would fly."[1] Tomb paintings in Egypt, Israel's great neighboring culture, show the deceased at work with his wife in the fields. This depiction, however, has nothing to do with the heavy labor of Egyptian peasants, but, instead, shows agriculture under paradisiacal conditions without sweat or strain. A similar view of work is also to be found in Genesis 2. Tilling and preserving the Garden of Eden makes the human being *homo faber*, the working being, whose status as a farmer is part of their condition. Only the of the fall and the ensuing punishment clearly shows how different the paradisiacal activity in the Garden of Eden was from the harsh reality beyond the garden's gates:

> And to the man [Adam] he said, "because you have listened to the voice of your wife, and have eaten of the tree about which I commanded you, 'You shall not eat of it,' cursed is the ground because of you; in toil you shall eat of it all the days of your life; thorns and thistles it shall bring forth for you; and you shall eat the plants of the field. By the sweat of your face you shall eat bread until you return to the ground, for out of it you were taken; you are dust, and to dust you shall return" (Gen 3:17–19).

The soil suffers the same fate as the serpent before it—both are cursed. Humanity and the serpent, the latter being seen here as a representative of undomesticated,

---

[1] Translator's note: cf. Martin Luther, "Treatise on Good Works (1520)," in Helmut T. Lehmann (ed.), *Luther's Works*, vol. 44 (Philadelphia: Fortress Press, 1966), 108.

dangerous animals, face each other as irreconcilable enemies. Man will strike the serpent's head, and the serpent will strike man's heel. The account of the fall can also be read as an etiological account giving answers to three questions:

- In the world created by God, why are there wild animals that present a danger to people?
- Why is giving birth a dangerous and painful process for women?
- Why must people work extremely hard to reap fruit from the ground given to them by God?

The Hebrew Bible often depicts birth as a moment of crisis (Gen 35:16–18; 1 Sam 4:19; Isa 42:14; Hos 13:13). There is much evidence of the existence of amulets, prayers, magic spells, etc. that were used for protection from the risks of giving birth in the region surrounding Israel. Such items seem to have been widespread as elements of personal piety in Israel. In the Hebrew Bible, YHWH occasionally appears as a birth attendant (Ps 22:10; 71:6). The account of the fall attempts to provide an explanation for the deficits with which humanity is confronted; the burdens of work and birth are part of humanity as God's creatures.

Numerous studies show that, in the preindustrial era, women's expertise in the preservation and processing of agricultural products was more pronounced and sophisticated than that of men. Indeed, in the story of Adam and Eve the role of women is not limited to childbearing, exempting them from work. Rather, the account's main purpose is to explain the travail of human existence. While men bear the burden of tilling the fields, women must endure the pains and dangers of bearing children:

> To the woman he [YHWH] said, "I will greatly increase your pangs in child-bearing; in pain you shall bring forth children, yet your desire shall be for your husband, and he shall rule over you" (Gen 3:16).

The translation proposed here does not understand pregnancy as an additional suffering women must endure, but rather as an explanation. This would suggest that the suffering connected with pregnancy and birth represent the overall plight of women. The text is also interesting in that it only mentions the sexual desire of women but, strangely enough, not that of men. This may mean that, despite the pains and dangers involved, women hold firmly to sexual desire and the wish to bear children.

In one respect, the penalty imposed on humankind is unclear: Adam, the human, has to bear the burden of work. But does this only refer to Adam the man? Or is Adam's wife, who is also a human being, subject to the heavy burden of work? Most, but not all, exegetes consider that men alone are subjected to the heavy burden of work. If this interpretation proved to be accurate, this would mean—at least according to the non-priestly prehistorical strands—that heavy physical labor is incompatible with creation theology's view of women.

## Two enemy brothers and the origin of the division of labor

The creation account about humanity's expulsion from paradise depicts people as farmers. The story of Cain and Abel paints a rather different picture, however, casting Abel as a livestock herder and Cain as a tiller of the soil (Gen 4:2). It is striking that precisely this division of labor introduces the diversity of humanity told in the narrative cycle, the individual stages of which are the creation of humanity, the expulsion from paradise, the flood and the Tower of Babel. Having recognized that this is an integral part of human prehistory is one of the great achievements of the authors of non-priestly prehistory. The story of Cain and Abel is a story of conflict; the central theme is enmity between two brothers, a theme that we also encounter in other biblical and ancient narratives. The brothers offer the fruits of their labor as a sacrifice before God; Cain offers the fruits of the soil, while Abel offers the firstborn of his sheep and goats and their "fat portions" (Gen 4:4). That YHWH accepts the shepherd's offerings, but rejects those of the farmer, is not to be understood as judgment for or against different lifestyles or types of nutrition. There is also no explanation as to how Cain realized that his sacrifice was not perfect. The account does not reveal why the work and the offering of one brother was accepted, while the other's was not. The consequences were catastrophic: the rejected farmer murdered his brother, the shepherd, and YHWH punishes him—henceforth the earth would withhold its produce from him and he would be doomed to the uncertain existence of a fugitive and wanderer. Cain's reaction is drastic:

> Cain said to the Lord, "My punishment is greater than I can bear! Today you have driven me away from the soil, and I shall be hidden from your face; I shall be a fugitive and a wanderer on the earth, and anyone who meets me may kill me" (Gen 4:14).

Cain's punishment was harsh. It is striking that he mentions the loss of his means of livelihood before mentioning his alienation from YHWH. Being driven from the soil and from being in YHWH's presence has two consequences for Cain: he is to live as a restless fugitive, moving through the land, exposed to the attacks of others. The only protection YHWH provides is the mark he places on him (Gen 4:15). Cain's story is thus not entirely over, as he finds a strategy against his lack of rest and employment.

"Cain knew his wife, and she conceived and bore Enoch; and he built a city, and named it Enoch after his son Enoch" (Gen 4:17). This verse poses difficult questions and challenges for exegetes. First of all, there is a contradiction in the fact that Cain goes from being a tiller of the soil to being a builder of cities. There is also no record of a city by the name of Enoch. Lastly, it is unusual to name a city after its founder's son rather than after its founder.

Despite such unresolved questions, one thing remains clear: the writer reveals a cultural and historical evolution from farmer to builder of cities. This does not mean that one form of living and working supplants the other, or that one is valued more highly than the other. The writer's main point in fact is the diversification of humanity. This becomes particularly clear in the way Cain's descendants are described. After a genealogy that moves from Enoch and Irad to Mehujael, Methushael and Lamech, Lamech's three sons are introduced. Jabel is presented as the father of all those who live in tents and have livestock, while his brother Jubal is the father of those who play the lyre and flute. The third brother, Tubal-cain, becomes the father of all those who make bronze and iron tools (Gen 4:20f.). The list does not presume to be complete, however. Nomads, musicians and smiths do not constitute the full spectrum of human activity. While Abel continued to be a herdsman of goats and sheep, the Hebrew term for large livestock, cattle in particular, in fact is used here. The three groups of people—nomadic shepherds, musicians and metalworkers—suggest a significant progress in the development of human culture. The ability to produce food, to pursue the arts and to work with metal constitutes a quantum leap in human development.

## Work and luxury—from farmer to winegrower

The story of the flood is followed by a short description of yet another cultural leap:

> Noah, a man of the soil, was the first to plant a vineyard. He drank some of the wine and became drunk, and he lay uncovered in his tent (Gen 9:20f.).

This episode seeks to tell us more than just about the introduction of viticulture and the perils of enjoying wine. Noah's son Ham, the father of Canaan, sees his father lying naked and reports the incident to his two brothers. This is dishonorable enough for Ham's son, Canaan, to be forced to carry Noah's curse.

Taken alone, Genesis 9:20 describes a progression from a culture of subsistence to a culture of pleasure. We must bear in mind, however, that excessive consumption of wine is only rarely criticized in the Hebrew Bible; other passages present the daily consumption of wine as quite normal (Gen 27:25; Judg 19:19; Isa 22:13).

It is surely not incidental to the narrative that Noah, the winegrower, does not sleep off his inebriation in a building but in a tent. Is this an indication of the arduousness of the work of the winegrower, with Noah having to keep watch over the fruits of his labor night and day?

Just as the account of the building of the Tower of Babel describes the human ability to collaborate on a large project, the account of Noah describes the ambivalence of the human ability to work generally. Even if his inebriation is not rebuked, the drunken, naked Noah lying in his tent is, in itself, something contemptible. In the Jewish exegesis of the Midrash (Bereshit Rabbah 32), the observation is made that Noah must logically have taken seedlings for grapevines and fig trees into the ark. Even if the modern interpretation rightly presumes that the tradition of Noah as a winegrower originally had nothing to do with the flood tradition, it nonetheless sees Noah as the custodian of a cultural technique. By transferring winemaking expertise to the new world, he provides the postdiluvian generations with a source of joy and celebration.

## "Come, let us build ourselves a city, and a tower." Work and the alienation from God

The building of the Tower of Babel is one of the best known accounts in the Bible. Throughout history, interpretations of the passage have generally focused on humanity's desire to be like God. This was the manifestation of a human hubris that YHWH could not leave unpunished. The history of art provides a great wealth of interpretations of the account, which can be summarized as "people running around in a vain attempt to conquer heaven." And yet, the biblical passage itself does not even say that it was people's goal to place themselves on an equal footing with God.

> Then they said, "Come, let us build ourselves a city, and a tower with its top in the heavens, and let us make a name for ourselves; otherwise we shall be scattered abroad upon the face of the whole earth" (Gen 11:4).

Up to this point there have only been accounts of the activity of individuals in biblical prehistory. Even the construction of the ark is the project of a single man. Genesis 11 speaks, for the first time, of a collective endeavor. The goal of making a name for oneself or creating a symbol that is visible from far and wide in order to prevent humanity from being scattered is never characterized as something reprehensible. More recent exegetes have categorically contested any form of human transgression in the construction account. The name Babel and the (archaeologically documented) construction of tall buildings there allude to its status as the political center of the entire world. Against this background, it has been suggested that the story is a critique of any attempt at world domination, as manifested in central, tall buildings and an (imposed) uniform language.

Despite any reservations about the fact that Genesis 11 does not specifically speak of human hubris, YHWH's intervention is a corrective and restrictive act, not a reaction against human construction projects. Humanity consequently becomes multilingual and is able to inhabit the entire world.

The story of the Tower of Babel is the first that speaks of humans working contrary to God's will. The ability to bake bricks and to coordinate the work of many people on a given building project constitutes a great achievement. The positive outcome of the account makes it clear that God's intervention is to be seen less as a punishment than as protection from an impending danger.

It is, however, still people's ability to work together on one project that sparked YHWH's intervention and the diversification of humanity. The passage would be essentially misunderstood if it were construed to convey a negative conception of work. Indeed, it does not deny that people can go to work willingly and, when possible, with enthusiasm. This is surprising since other ancient Middle Eastern writings provide examples of the negative side of construction work, as in the Babylonian epic of Atrahasis:

> When the gods were man
> they did forced labor, they bore drudgery.
> Great indeed was the drudgery of the gods,
> the forced labor was heavy, the misery too much.[2]

This negative attitude toward work can also be readily found in Greek literature, and it is striking that the Hebrew Bible does not include any negative perceptions of physical labor. Even the Shabbat commandment to rest on the seventh day of the week does not aim at satisfying the human need for a day of freedom from work. Instead, it places a limitation on the human need to work. The imposed abstention from work is justified from the point of view

---

[2] *The Epic of Atrahasis*, at **www.livius.org/as-at/atrahasis/atrahasis.html** .

of both creation theology and liberation theology. The Exodus version of the Decalogue justifies the Shabbat commandment on the basis of the Creator's rest (Ex 20:11). In Deuteronomy, on the other hand, the Decalogue justifies the right of the indentured to a day of rest because of the Israelite's experience as slaves in Egypt (Deut 5:15).

The account of the Tower of Babel brings biblical prehistory to a conclusion. It is the relentless efforts of a united humanity on a common construction project that leads YHWH to act. It is not human hubris, as is often asserted, but the concern that human unity could allow people to implement any conceivable plan (Gen 11:6) that forces YHWH to act. It would seem here that working on one and the same project would lead humanity to uniformity. The world's ethnic and linguistic diversity is the consequence of YHWH's intervention—and is thus both a blessing and a rescue from harm.

## Work and creation: an overview

Work is part of humanity's condition as God's creature. In paradise, people were called to perform (effortless) work for its own sake. By disobeying God's commandment not to eat of the fruit of the Tree of Knowledge, people were not, as it is often incorrectly asserted, punished by having to work.[3] YHWH's curse in fact falls on the ground and turns human work into a burden.

Non-priestly prehistory describes work as a human characteristic, of being the *homo faber* who does not engage in work for the sake of God or in place of God, but for his own sake. Since creation theology defines work as a part of being human, one can—from a modern perspective—infer that the right to work exists. If, accordingly, people can be conceived of as nothing other than a creature that works, deprivation or curtailment of work is tantamount to a curtailment of being fully human.

According to the witness of biblical prehistory, work, success and election by God are not necessarily intertwined. The destiny of Cain, who attempts to offer YHWH the products of his toil in vain, shows that successful work or business must not be misunderstood as a sign of divine election. The Book of Ecclesiastes goes a step beyond this by calling into question the usefulness of human work in general.

The society depicted in the prehistorical genealogies is characterized by a division of labor. The categorization of humanity into the three major groups

---

[3] Cf. Luther, *WA* 6, 271:35: "We were then all sentenced to work in Adam."

of shepherds, musicians and craftsmen (Gen 4:20–22) serves to illustrate that, from the perspective of the theology of creation, all human work activities are to be understood as stemming from humankind's condition. It is noteworthy that the burden of physical work is only placed on the man (Adam), whereas the woman must bear the burden and danger connected with giving birth.

Work can lead to the alienation from God. Even if the Tower of Babel account does not explicitly say what is wrong with the collective decision to build a city and a tower; the culmination of this collective work project is human alienation from God. Because this case involves a particular form of human work and activity that ultimately proves to be destructive, it does not depreciate human work *per se*.

# Work in the New Testament and in Greco-Roman Antiquity

### Christoph vom Brocke

## Introduction

For many years the topic of "work" lurked in the shadows of biblical scholarship. It was the long-term unemployment situation in central Europe that began in the 1980s and the social problems it caused that sparked renewed theological interest in this subject. In particular, it became the focus of so-called sociohistorical research represented by New Testament scholars such as Gerd Theißen, Luise Schottroff and Wolfgang Stegemann adding to the corpus of New Testament exegesis.

Meanwhile, the phenomenon of mass unemployment did not spare the African continent: in many countries of Africa high unemployment among youth especially is becoming a serious problem. Not to mention the problem posed by a shift in the work ethos under the influence of the Western way of life and the concomitant decline of traditional African values.

Against this background, we might ask ourselves again what insights the Bible, the New Testament, in particular, can contribute on the subject.

## The Bible in general

First of all, there is no general "biblical doctrine" of work. The various references to it are disparate and date from diverse epochs. Moreover, work for subsistence is never uplifted theologically, as it would be later on with Martin Luther, who saw in daily work a particular form of worship.

What can be said, nonetheless, is that in both the Old and the New Testament, work in the sense of gainful employment is seen as something that is self-evidently inherent to human existence and given by God. The first chapters of the Bible, recounting how God placed the human being in the Garden of Eden to "till it and keep it," attest to this.

In other words, paradise was not a place in which the fruits of the earth virtually fell into one's mouth or one merely had to stoop to gather them. On the contrary, even in the Garden of Eden, having to work is one of the natural conditions of human existence. The obligation to work, therefore, is not a consequence of original sin as is repeatedly asserted, but, rather, a fact of life dating back to the very beginning.

What changed because of sin and the ensuing curse is merely the fact that the ground that humans cultivate yields its fruit only after great effort and great human input. The ground is cursed, but not work *per se* (Gen 3:17).

That (manual) labor is a self-evident fact of human existence runs through the Bible like a golden thread—from the Book of Genesis to John's Apocalypse. Even in the last book of the Bible it is not at all foreseen that the people of the heavenly Jerusalem will lapse into complete idleness, but rather that they will be occupied in serving God (Rev 22:3).

From a biblical point of view, we can therefore affirm that there is no life without work. This does not imply that, conversely, life only exists through work.[1] Even though Martin Luther's statement that "As the bird is born to fly, so is man born to work"[2] appears—from a human point of view—to be logical, it is not mentioned in the Bible.

Since human labor is indissociable from the "sweat of one's face" (Gen 3:19) the Bible recognizes—no doubt as an attenuation—the pattern of the seven-day week, at the end of which comes the Sabbath when all work ceases. This rule comes from God, who rested after completing the work of creation ("and he rested on the seventh day from all the work he had done" Gen 2:2).

There has never been a consensus among Jews as to how strictly the interdiction of work on the Sabbath should be interpreted and what types of work are allowed on the Sabbath. This is illustrated in Jesus' discussions about the question of the Sabbath in the gospels (cf. Mk 2f.).

Early Christianity did not take over the law of the Sabbath; to some extent it even criticized it as idleness. However, the Sunday rest was introduced partly as a substitute for the Sabbath rest, applying initially only to the time for worship. Under the first Christian emperor Constantine I, (†337 AD), an imperial decree made Sunday a general day of rest throughout the empire.

---

[1] Cf. J. Ebach, "Labor II. Bible," in *Religion Past and Present*, vol. 7 (2010), 271. Cf. also Nikolaus Count von Zinzendorf († 1760), founder of the Moravian Brotherhood, who reportedly said: "We live to work."

[2] Martin Luther, "Treatise on Good Works (1520)," in Helmut T. Lehmann (ed.), *Luther's Works*, vol. 44 (Philadelphia: Fortress Press, 1966), 108.

## Greco-Roman antiquity

### *The ideal image of the work of free citizens*

Greco-Roman society did not share the biblical view that labor (manual labor, in particular) was a fundamental characteristic of human existence. Although one must be careful not to generalize, it is clear that in the period from Plato (fourth century BC) to Cicero (first century BC), from Greek to Roman antiquity, work—physical work especially—was considered to be a matter for slaves, not for free citizens.

This phenomenon accompanied the emergence of democracy as a form of government in the sixth and fifth centuries BC already, particularly in Athens. *De facto*, this means that the active participation by free citizens in the administration of the city-state (*polis*) was needed, especially the holding of regular political office. Such time-intensive responsibilities were understandably quite incompatible with gainful employment. This, with time, led to the ideal image of a free citizen who did not depend on income produced by the work of his own hands, but rather, was able to use others (mainly slaves) to work for him, while he in his leisure time took an active part in the political activities of his city. This principle was already applied at the time of the Greek philosopher Aristotle (†322 BC) in the fourth century BC and was later cultivated by the Romans, the most prominent example of which is the rhetorician and statesman Marcus Tullius Cicero (†43 BC).

In Rome one relied on employees or slaves to perform manual work in the literal sense. Free Roman citizens engaged in sports and occupied themselves with politics, philosophy or other so-called liberal arts *(artes liberales)*. In the first century AD, it was even the rule in Rome that no one actively exercising a profession could hold a political office. While "leisure" *(otium)* characterized the free Roman citizen, "work" fell on the non-free population and the subjugated peoples of the provinces.

It should not be forgotten that this ideal only applied to the Roman upper class, which lived on income from its lands. The vast majority of the population had to rely on "normal" income-generating activities in trade and commerce as merchants, craftsmen and manual workers. The daily lives of the lower class composed of slaves, wage earners and small tenants were far more wearisome and physically demanding, especially for those occupied in agriculture, where the days were long and the work hard. This was especially true in the case of large landed estates—the so-called latifundia—on which slaves and day laborers, supervised by imperial officials, eked out a meager existence.

Equally notorious and feared was the work in mines and quarries, relying on the forced labor of slaves and prisoners of war. The situation of the popular masses, therefore, differed radically from that of the upper class. In addition, while in antiquity daily hard work was a bitter reality for the vast majority of people, the trades in "which one earned one's meager daily bread with one's own hands were generally despised by the aristocracy."[3]

Typical of this aristocratic narrow-mindedness is the famous passage from Cicero's De officiis,[4] where he speaks disparagingly of all trades that involve physical labor, for this, in his view, was in fact the work of slaves. Other commercial professions and crafts fare equally badly with him. Only the professions that require an elevated, intellectual education, as for example, doctors, architects or wholesale traders, receive better consideration. The acme as far as Cicero is concerned, however, is land ownership, which allows one to reply on the work of others.

### Income differences

Income differences give an idea of the magnitude of the gap separating the Roman upper class and the working population, especially landless day laborers: taking Matthew 20:2, "After agreeing with the laborers for the usual daily wage [i.e., one denarius], he sent them into his vineyards," as a reference one may assume that a Roman denarius was roughly equivalent to the sum that a day laborer could expect as a wage.[5] This would amount to an annual income of around 100 denarii, for the day laborer cannot expect to find work every day, but primarily only during the planting and harvesting seasons. In contrast, the wage for a simple scribe was around two to three denarii a day. A regular activity could bring in between 500 and 1,000 denarii a year.

The annual income of a member of the Roman upper class, as for example that of Lucius Iunius Gallio, the proconsul of the province of Achaia mentioned in Acts 18:12, was situated at around 250,000 denarii. The income of the Pontius Pilate of the Passion account must not have been much less. Even a normal middle-class free citizen in Rome enjoyed an annual income of 5,000 denarii, that is, fifty times more that of a day laborer in the farms of the Roman provinces.

---

[3] Martin Hengel, "Die Arbeit im frühen Christentum" [Work in early Christianity], in Theologische Beiträge 17 (1986), 176.

[4] "On Duties," at www.stoics.com/cicero_book.html#Trade1.

[5] Hengel, op. cit. (note 3), 185, considers the sum of one denarius quoted in Mt 20:2 as an "ideal," the real wage being markedly lower.

### *The influence of the Greco-Roman ideal image*

The Book of Sirach—an apocryphal Jewish work of the second century BC—gives an indication of the extent to which Cicero's ideal image of the Greco-Roman upper class was accepted by society and how strong its influence was among Jews. While the Hebrew Bible, specifically the Book of Psalms, acknowledges the hardship of manual work, especially in agriculture,[6] but does not have a negative perception of it, here we find a statement saying that only those who are free of toil can be wise or become scribes. Farmers, shepherds and other craftsmen are not suitable to this (Sir 38:24ff.). "This contempt for physical work among the ruling class of the Greco-Roman and Jewish societies"[7] does not agree with the overall witness of the Old Testament and eventually must have clashed with early Christianity, which primarily presented itself as a movement of simple folk among whom the fact of earning one's livelihood with one's own hands was implicitly accepted. In fact, the figureheads of this movement such as Jesus himself were craftsmen, some disciples were simple fishermen and the apostle to the Gentiles, Paul, also worked with his hands. So it is no wonder that, in the second century AD, learned philosophers such as Celsus made fun of Christians because they were merely primitive, uneducated people, simple craftsmen or tillers of the soil.[8] Even if these reproaches appear somewhat exaggerated, they touch the core of the question: early Christians were nearly automatically members of the working population.

## Jesus and Paul on work

In contrast to the Greco-Roman upper class, neither Jesus nor Paul made disparaging statements in relation to physical labor. Both remain firmly within the tradition of the Old Testament and rabbinic Judaism of their time. Whereas the Old Testament, especially the parts devoted to wisdom, admonishes against laziness and its consequences (Prov 6:6f.; 10:4; 12:27 etc.), the Judaism of the time of the New Testament actually insists on the obligation to work physically. For example, it was the rule that the education of scribes include the learning of a craft. Genesis 2:15 tells us that the human is obliged

---

[6] Cf. Ps 104:23.

[7] Hengel, op. cit. (note 3), 178.

[8] Cf. Origen, *Contra Celsus* 3:55, at **www.earlychristianwritings.com/text/origen163.html**.

to work (manually).[9] The combination of intellectual and physical work was perceived as an ideal. There is the well-known dictum by Gamaliel III, a great third-century rabbi, who is supposed to have said: "Beautiful is the study of the Torah with the way of the world."[10] In some respects, the apostle Paul, who was a former Pharisee and scribe (Phil 3:5) and who had learned and exercised the trade of a tentmaker (Acts 18:3), fit this ideal, as did Jesus himself. When he was respected as "rabbi" (Mk 9:5; 10:51; etc.)—although we are not aware that he had studied the Torah—"this double profession would correspond to rabbinic tradition whereby all rabbis also had a trade."[11]

## *Jesus—builder and artisan of the kingdom of God*

Jesus, son of Joseph, was a builder by trade—the term "carpenter" ("Is this not the carpenter?" Mk 6:3) does not correctly render the τέκτων of the Greek text. As far as we know, however, he no longer exercised this trade during his days as an itinerant preacher in Galilee. For one thing, this is clearly due to the fact that a builder presumably would need a workshop, since the tools required for working with wood as well as stone are only partially transportable.

For another, with Jesus, the concept of work undergoes a transformation involving a complete reevaluation and eclipsing the fundamentally positive attitude toward gainful employment. Of course, Jesus himself was well aware of the hardships of the working world in all its facets, as the numerous references in the parables show—the difficulties encountered by farmers when sowing their seed (Mk 4); or when having to struggle with crop failures and weeds (Mt 13); fishermen who cast their nets all night long to no avail (Lk 5), shepherds in the mountains of Palestine (Lk 15); and the joblessness of day laborers who in vain seek work in the vineyards (Mt 20). None of this was unfamiliar to Jesus and, yet, this was not his message. Rather, he set great store by the proclamation of the coming of the reign of God. This also had implications for his conception of work. For him work is not merely manual labor, but, first and foremost, the commitment to the kingdom of God. Jesus gives up his work as a builder in exchange for that of an itinerant preacher for the kingdom of God. The apostles Peter and Andrew, John and James, too, and even the tax collectors Levi (Mk 2:14) and Matthew (Mt 9:9), were called to abandon their normal existence to serve the kingdom of God, leaving behind

---

[9] Cf. Hengel, op. cit. (note 3), 184.

[10] Wolfgang Schrage, "Ethik des Neuen Testaments" [New Testament Ethics], in *NTD* Expanded Series 4 (Göttingen: Vandenhoeck and Ruprecht, 1989), 238.

[11] Karl Hermann Schelkle, "Art. Arbeit III. Neues Testament," in *TRE3* (1978), 622.

their trades to become fishers of people, "Follow me and I will make you fish for people" (Mk 1:17). This transformation process of the concept of work is also to be found in the introductory passage of the great commission, "The harvest is plentiful, but the laborers are few; therefore ask the Lord of the harvest to send out laborers into his harvest" (Lk 10:2f.).

This new labor as fishers of people or, here, as harvesters, is by no means a sinecure. It is marked by rejection and hostility, and is not even remunerated, at least not with money.[12] But it stands under the promise of the goodness of God who cares for God's laborers. This is what the statement, "The laborer deserves to be paid" (Lk 10:7) really means. God will open people's hearts so that they welcome God's messengers and care for their basic needs.

This is how Jesus' bidding in the Sermon on the Mount is to be understood, "So do not worry about tomorrow, for tomorrow will bring worries of its own. Today's trouble is enough for today" (Mt 6:34).

Jesus directs the attention of his listeners to nature, to the birds of the air, to the lilies of the field that do not work and yet do not want, for they live on the goodness of God who provides for them. These words seem almost to contradict the Old Testament wisdom whereby the industriousness of the ants is given as an example to the lazy, the insouciant: "Go to the ant, you lazybones; consider its ways, and be wise" (Prov 6:6).

But Jesus is not talking about careless "workaphobia" nor advocating idleness, but rather, he is calling for trust in God's goodness. Daily work is necessary precisely because of the knowledge that God is the Father who knows what is essential for existence and who will provide for God's children. This reduces the pressure to grant too much importance in life to daily gainful employment. It is not without good reason that Jesus cites the rich farmer who made his work and income the center of his existence as a negative, dissuasive example (cf. Lk 12:16ff.). Jesus' harsh reaction to the overly busy Martha is to be understood in the same way.[13] For those who followed him, Jesus' message about the imminence of the kingdom of God constituted a radical interruption of the normal daily work routine, but did not alter the external conditions. Jesus was not a social revolutionary who sought to change the prevailing social order for the benefit of

---

[12] In this regard, Mark 10:28ff. is interesting; here Peter (as spokesperson for the disciples) raises the question of the reward for having abandoned their families and the loss of their social security ("Look we have left everything and followed you"). Here it is clear that the disciples' new occupation as fishers of people does not render the question of remuneration superfluous. The reward promised by Jesus ("There is no one who ... will not receive a hundredfold") is shifted to a different level. Just as the concept of work is transformed by Jesus into work for the kingdom of God, the concept of reward is similarly transformed.

[13] Cf. Lk 10:41, "Martha, Martha, you are worried and distracted by many things; there is need of only one thing."

the poor. Rather, he focused on the trust in the benevolent heavenly father that liberates from compulsive anxiety over material survival and places daily work and effort in the hands of God. Jesus' own life as an itinerant preacher without social security and that of his apostles are sufficiently good examples of this.

In this regard, the short passage in Luke 8:3 is interesting; it describes a circle of followers of Jesus beyond the twelve apostles who provided for the daily subsistence of the whole group out of their resources. The fact that Jesus and his disciples were able to give up their trades is therefore also thanks to wealthy backers such as Joanna, the wife of Herod's steward, who devoted their money to God's cause.

### Paul—missionary and tentmaker

With Paul, we find very similar views on work to those of Jesus. He likewise refers to his dedication to spreading the Good News as work—hard work and effort, that often demanded a very high commitment on his part. He himself states that he worked harder than the other apostles: "I worked harder than any of them" (1 Cor 15:10); this is probably based on genuine fact because, in contrast to Jesus and the disciples, we know that Paul exercised his tentmaker trade in parallel with his missionary activity (Acts 18:3). Acts 18:1–3, for example, recounts that, in Corinth, Paul worked with Aquila and Priscilla, who were also tentmakers and had preceded him to Corinth from Rome.

Paul had the great advantage of being able to exercise his trade during his travels. The tools he needed to do all types of leather work were transportable and could comfortably fit into a rucksack.

The tenacity with which Paul, during his missionary voyages, coped with the dual task of proclaiming the gospel and exercising his manual trade, requiring sometimes even to work nights—"We worked night and day" (1 Thess 2:9)—is remarkable.

Of course, he could have let the churches provide for him; according to early Christian standards, he certainly would have had that right (1 Cor 9:14f.). He does not avail himself of this, however, not wanting to give the impression of making the "Word of God" a business. This is understandable when one considers that larger cities in the Roman Empire, such as Corinth, constantly attracted numerous orators and itinerant philosophers who, for a fee, would deliver fine speeches for any occasion. Paul did not in any way want to be confused with this kind of competition. He thus worked very hard to earn his livelihood and renounced his right to remuneration—which, on the other hand, exposed him to being reproached for lacking apostolic authority (1 Cor 9:1–4).

Also to be noted is that Paul found himself in permanent financial difficulty. Travel was very costly, and ship passages were particularly expensive. In addition, his collaborators—who were always with him—wanted to be provided for. This gave rise to a permanent need to pursue regular gainful employment. Paul often complained about the daily struggle to provide for themselves: "To the present hour we are hungry and thirsty ... and homeless, and we grow weary from the work of our own hands" (1 Cor 4:11f.). Of course, churches here and there participated financially (Phil 2:25; 4:16), but that was not the rule.

However, Paul also recognized in gainful employment the advantage of financial independence, which was a fitting example for the churches. For example, he reminded the church in Thessalonika that they had to earn their livelihood with their own hands in order to earn the respect of outsiders and to depend on no one: "... aspire to live quietly, to mind your own affairs, and to work with your hands, as we directed you, so that you may behave properly toward outsiders and be dependent on no one" (1 Thess 4:11f.).

### Work and social responsibility

The notion that regular gainful employment ensures charitable activities and social responsibility on the part of the church still does not yet explicitly appear here. Yet, one should remember that the admonitions in 1 Thessalonians 4:11 "to work with your hands" come under the category of "love of the brothers and sisters" (1 Thess 4:9).

This principle is formulated very clearly in the later Letter to the Ephesians, which presumably was not written by Paul himself, but by one of his disciples. Here the foundations of an "early Christian social ethic"[14] are outlined for the first time in the history of Christianity. Ephesians 4:28 reads: "Thieves must give up stealing; rather let them labor and work honestly with their own hands, so as to have something to share with the needy." Accordingly, Christians must engage in regular work in order to be able to share their earned income with others.

Already in the Old Testament, providing for the poor was an important obligation that differentiated Jews from their neighbors. With its emphasis on the commandment of love, it became, in early Christianity, to a certain extent the hallmark by which the new religion was recognized by others.

This notion of providing for the poor stands implicitly behind the Greek churches' collection, organized by Paul for the poor in Jerusalem. For Paul,

---

[14] Hengel, op. cit. (note 3), 201.

establishing the necessary equality between those who have and those who have not as an obvious work of active charity: "it is a question of a fair balance between your present abundance and their need, so that their abundance may be for your need" (2 Cor 8:13f.).

The collection, which had been agreed to at the council of the year 48/49 AD (Gal 2:10), was possible because the Paulinian churches in Greece, who were to bear the brunt of the burden, were financially able to do so, thanks to their regular income from work. The fact that Paul had to exhort the Corinthians several times (2 Cor 8) and even suggested that on the first day of the week, i.e., Sunday, a small sum be set aside (1 Cor 16:1f.) allows one to conclude that it was not easy for churches to take part in the collection. It may be assumed that only the regular, gainful employment of their members guaranteed the success of the collection (Rom 16:26).

### *Theologically motivated neglect of work*

In early Christendom, there were frequent cases of theologically motivated idleness, which led to the neglect of everyday tasks and abandonment of work. Already 2 Thessalonians, which is considered by most exegetes not to be by Paul, addresses this problem. This explains the harsh reproof to the church:

> Anyone unwilling to work should not eat. For we hear that some of you are living in idleness, mere busybodies, not doing any work. Now such persons we command and exhort in the Lord Jesus Christ to do their work quietly and to earn their own living (2 Thess 3:10-12).

> This brusque sounding command shows how great was the temptation on the part of early Christians—out of zeal and eschatological motives—to abandon a difficult job, not only in the years immediately following the enthusiastic experience of the latter-day spirit, but even decades later.[15]

Expecting the imminent second coming of Christ (*parousia*) led to neglecting the tasks of everyday life. When the Lord comes again, all earthly conditions will, in any case, be fulfilled, so that already in the present, it no longer makes sense to engage in arduous daily work. In fact, regular work could be an obstacle to preparations for the reunion with the coming Lord (cf. Mt 25:1–13).

---

[15] Ibid., 199.

Or perhaps the "Do not worry" from Jesus' Sermon on the Mount (Mt 6:34) was simply misinterpreted by some, leading them to neglect daily work.[16] When Jesus extolled the lilies of the fields, who neither toil nor worry about their day-to-day attire but yet are splendidly clothed (Mt 6:28), should that not apply all the more to human beings?

In contrast, Paul and his disciples' insistent emphasis on gainful employment in no way implies neglect of manual labor. On the contrary, in their view, daily gainful employment not only guarantees one's own subsistence and independence, but also enables one to engage in solidarity actions for the benefit of brothers and sisters in the body of Christ who are in want.

## Post-New Testament perspectives

The emphasis on the obligation to work and the social responsibility aspect of work observed in Paul's own writings and in the later (deutero-) Pauline letters is even more apparent in the writings of the Apostolic Fathers (first/second centuries AD).[17] For example, the "Shepherd of Hermas (circa 140 AD) praises the believers who always have "pity on every man" and give "aid from their own labor",[18] while the "Letter of Barnabas" (130-140 AD) likewise exhorts to working with one's hands and to generosity and willingness to give—not omitting to mention the redeeming action of work.[19]

Since there apparently was repeated abuse of Christian generosity, particularly with regard to hospitality, the "Didache" (circa 100 AD) urges that a traveling brother not be received for more than two or three days. If he stays longer, he must work.[20]

What is most striking is the fact that many churches regarded it their duty to provide suitable employment for their members (Did 12:6), if they became jobless. Every person should work and earn money, not only in order to provide for themselves, but also to care for needy brothers (and sisters). Here a completely new problem arose in the case of Christians who had to give up their traditional line of work because of their faith. There were many such professions in the

---

[16] According to Detlev Dormeyer et al. (eds), "Arbeit in der Antike, in Judentum und Christentum" [Work in antiquity, Judaism and Christianity], in *Münsteraner Judaistische Studien*, vol. 20 (Berlin: Lit Verlag, 2006), 102.

[17] Cf. hereafter Hengel, op. cit. (note 3), 202ff.

[18] Ninth Similitude, chapter 24, at **www.newadvent.org/fathers/02013.htm.**

[19] Barnabas 19:10–11, at **www.earlychristianwritings.com/text/barnabas-lightfoot.html.**

[20] Did 12:4ff., at **www.earlychristianwritings.com/text/didache-lightfoot.html**

second century. The list of trades considered to be "unchristian" was long and did not only involve soldiers, gladiators and other athletes, but all professions through which, to some extent or other, one came into contact with pagan beliefs. These included public officials, astrologers, painters, sculptors, actors, teachers, architects etc. For all of these, the church attempted to provide suitable support. If suitable employment could not be secured, the means of subsistence were provided, as far as this was possible. This is particularly the case of those who for some reason could not work at all: widows, orphans, elderly or sick slaves and virgins living ascetic lives.

There also appeared to be some kind of assistance provided for setting up a business to allow Christians who wanted to become independent to engage in a new career.

The extensive resonance given to the subject by pagan writers indicates to what extent charitable and socially committed activities were a distinctive characteristic of congregations in the Early Church. Although Christians were often criticized or ridiculed, their hard work together with their social commitment earned them great respect.

## Conclusion

Overall the development in early Christianity from Paul and the Letter to the Ephesians through the Apostolic Fathers gives a very clear picture of the understanding of work: work is not a goal in itself, but a necessary activity whose objective it is to ensure one's own livelihood and to succor—when necessary—neighbors in need. It is precisely this aspect that differentiated early Christianity from its Greco-Roman context.

However, the emphasis on work as an obligation should not become some kind of theological exaggeration as is the case in certain Calvinistic traditions for example: the Jesuanic "do not worry" is not compatible either with the theologization of work as a sign of divine election or with a unilateral stylization of work as the service to others. Jesus' clear witness with his rejection of human efforts to place gainful employment in the center of existence precludes a priori any theological or ideological over-ladening of the New Testament concept.

# An African Theology of Work: A Lutheran Perspective

## Kenneth Mtata

To try and give an account of the theology of work from an African Lutheran perspective can only be a limited exercise. In the first place, Africa is too large to have its views represented by a single perspective. In all modesty, by "African" I refer only to one view of Africa, one from the Mberengwa district in the midlands of Zimbabwe, a place comprising a mixture of the Karanga and Ndebele ethnic groups. This region of Mberengwa, linked with Beitbridge and Gwanda in Matebeleland south, is predominantly Lutheran as a result of the dominant presence of the Swedish missionaries, who, in 1903, started their missionary work in Zimbabwe. The people living in this area share some commonalities with other Africans that can be safely used to develop a theology of work that is genuinely African. The second challenge is that even though I write as a Lutheran, talking in terms of denomination in Africa is superficial since categories such as Lutheran, Methodist, or Catholic matter more to the clergy than they do to the ordinary Christian. Denominational identities take other forms and doctrinal differences are rarely important in defining them. Since the work of Swedish Lutheran missionaries informs part of the discussion, I shall keep this Lutheran perspective while keeping the above in mind. The third challenge is that Africa has been and is changing. Therefore, any fair account of the African understanding of work will take these changes seriously, especially since they influenced certain directions with regard to thinking about work. In the following, I shall take the precolonial, colonial and postcolonial epochs as categories for discussing the changing African perspectives on work and examine how a contemporary theology of work could be developed in light of these changes. Although they overlap, I shall look at these epochs separately so as to understand the changes. My main focus will be the precolonial views and how these were reshaped in the context of colonialism and missionary activity.

## A precolonial African view of work

In its early phases, African theology was rightly accused of nostalgic reconstructions of the traditional Africa. While this accusation is true, I believe that whenever we reconstruct, we do not exclude the ideal from the reconstruction. The past is not just past facts; it is a reconstruction informed by the hope of its inspiring the future. How did Africans understand work before they encountered other cultures? Having left very little for us to work with—Africa was an oral rather than a literate culture—we can only glean from some practices that remain in the form of rituals and the accounts of Western writers. We therefore need to tread cautiously here. What we can observe from African languages shows that Africans had a particular view of totality regarding work and other spheres of life. Apart from being a means toward an end, namely sustenance, work was part and parcel of life, ritually organized around the agricultural cycles. Among the Bantu languages one can discern this inseparable link between religious ritual and ordinary work. Words such as *basa* in Shona, *umsebenz*[1] in Xhosa/Zulu or Ndebele, denote cultural traditional rituals associated with ancestral veneration, burial, or other traditional religious practices to "secure" the home, in addition to referring to ordinary household or homestead chores. As the German missionary Theo Sundermeier, who resided in several countries in southern Africa suggests, according to this understanding, work as ritual plays a role more central to traditional African religion than religious contemplation.[2] It is with reference to the ubiquitous presence of religion in the day-to-day lives of Africans that we can understand John Mbiti's well-known opening statement, "Africans are notoriously religious."[3] In ritual, Africans express their deep convictions about work that were passed on from generation to generation so that every ritual moment was a moment of apprenticeship, where the younger generation was initiated into all the professions central to their lives; the life of work was ordered and regulated by rituals. Since traditional African societies were largely agrarian, such work and the rituals circumscribing it were enacted in synchrony with the changing agricultural seasons of rainmaking, sowing, thanksgiving, harvesting, thanksgiving and so on. Within this cycle or cycles other tasks were performed, whose function was to service the cycles and to allow for the creativity that colored the routines of the agricultural cycle in addition to the basic purpose of basic sustenance (food, water, shelter and life rituals). The religious nature of work meant that Africans experienced work mainly as a collective at two levels.

---

[1] Mark B. Watson and Graham B. Stead, "Contextual Transformation and the Career Development of Black South African Youth," in Christopher R. Stones (ed.), *Socio-political and Psychological Perspectives in South Africa* (New York: Nova Science Press, 2001), 173–95, here 184, for Xhosa descriptions.

[2] Theo Sundermeier, *The Individual and Community in African Traditional Religions* (Hamburg: LIT, 1998), 53.

[3] John Mbiti, *African Religions and Philosophy* (New York: Praeger Publishers, 1969), 1.

## Work with others

At one level, in traditional African societies work was accomplished by groups of people working together, usually with the household constituting a production unit. This resulted in the significance of having many children and hence many wives. Moreover, to consolidate resources, the communities usually pulled together the different family production units into one big unit to work in rotation on each other's fields. Among the Shona of Zimbabwe, it was common to invite neighbors to a task at a gathering called *humwe* (unity) or *nhimbe*, a practice that is still current today in some parts of Zimbabwe. This meant that much work could be done within a short space of time.

Since work had to be done with others, relationships were built into the labor practices. In this sense, work was part and parcel of the larger system of relationship building. A very good example is the practice of *kutema ugariri*. Let me cite an example reminiscent of the story of Jacob's marriage to Leah and Rachael in Genesis 29. If a man of limited means wanted to get married but could not raise the bride price, then he would spend time working in his future father-in-law's homestead before being given his wife and, usually in addition, a few animals and utensils. Establishing a relationship in this way also assured the bride's parents that the bridegroom's work ethic would sustain the needs of his family. These marriage systems served other purposes too, but this is not our concern here.[4]

## Individual work

While individuality was submerged in such highly developed networks of relationships, it was not completely obliterated. First, individuals were marked by their tools. It was believed that a tool, once mixed with the worker's sweat, lost its neutrality as an object. It had become part and parcel of the person and could only be used by others after an appropriate ritual had been performed. Its properties were transformed and charged with personal aspects. So even in the same family there was a hoe for each person, a knob carry for each person, a spear for each person. People could not share these without observing the appropriate ritual protocol, since there was a basic understanding regarding the sacredness of persons, their discharge (sweat and saliva), which could be

---

[4] Gerald Chikozho Mazarire, "Reflections on Pre-colonial Zimbabwe, c. 850–880s," in Brian Raftopoulos and Alois Mlambo (eds), *Becoming Zimbabwe: A History from the Pre-Colonial Period to 2008* (Harare: Weaver Press, 2009), 1–38, here 13.

passed on through the use of the same tools. This has lived on until today. I remember that when my uncle, who was a bus driver, had an accident there was much talk in the family about the fact that the seat and the steering wheel used by the previous driver had not been ritually cleansed before he had assumed the position as the new driver. This association of tools with individuals is also evident in such objects as office chairs, bus seats, etc. Even in modern day Zimbabwe it is not common to enter another person's office and sit on their official chair. This sacredness of the person had negative effects in that it was hierarchical. Everything was sacred but their levels of sacredness differed.

Second, individual work was also recognized through individual exploits. Names still exist for those individuals known for their excellence in certain areas of work. For example, the Shona *mhizha*, were known for their craftsmanship, *hombarume* for their hunting skills, and the *hurudza* for their farming prowess. Even those members of the community renowned for their lack of industry had names reserved for them. The Shona words *vusimbe* and *nungo,* literally weak bones or laziness, are old terms used to describe those unwilling to work. This was a great weakness since it was considered to be the cause of poverty and could lead one to becoming a *mupemhi* (beggar), a disgrace according to African thinking.[5] Even though laziness was directly associated with poverty, this way of thinking was almost neutralized by the belief that no matter how well one worked, one's work would not amount to anything without the blessings of the gods. This leads us to look at another level of the collective nature of work.

## Work and the spiritual world

Whether the hunter had good dogs, the farmer had many cattle to plough the field, or one had a great voice to sing, in order to be successful in one's work, Africans believed in the final capital that came from the spiritual world, be they ancestors or God or other benevolent powers. Excelling individuals were not always credited for their industry but rather for their spiritual resource and hence the need to perform rituals before, during and after their work. For example, productivity of the land alone could not be guaranteed by the fertility of the soil, sufficient rain and one's farming skills alone. In the Shona tradition for instance one needed traditional medicines such as *divisi,* a potion believed to influence productivity.[6] Based on their divination, specialists could advise on

---

[5] Michael Gelfand, *Diet and Tradition in an African Culture* (London: E & S Livingston, 1971), 22.

[6] János M. Bak and Gerhard Benecke (eds), *Religion and Rural Revolt* (Manchester: Manchester University Press, 1982), 317.

agricultural issues since they knew what crop would be suitable for a particular season. The same was true for the chief, who could not rule alone, even if he had inherited his chieftaincy. He needed *kuromba* (to strengthen himself). In traditional Zimbabwe, and even today, those in positions of power are known to go to a diviner who will ritually strengthen their position of power and help them fend off anyone intending to usurp their position. The traditional chief needed the help of mediums when making decisions and to ensure that his office was secure. Without such a medium no chief could feel safe enough to rule. According to this understanding, work is the cooperation between human beings and the spiritual world.

## Work and rest

Having worked hard throughout the day with the help of the God, traditional African societies spent the evening around the fire, resting and telling stories; resting and leisure were inscribed in the life of work. It is surprising that even today some Western scholars claim that "...leisure was a concept alien to Africa... ."[7] Everyone who has been to Africa knows that Africans are known for their sense of celebration and joyfulness. Africans intensely celebrated their life and work long before they encountered other cultures and, in traditional Zimbabwean society for instance, one day a week was known as *chisi*, a day of rest. This was not a fixed day since usually the local chief prescribed the *chisi* because a death had occurred in the region or because the mediums had recommended rest during the rainmaking sessions.[8] *Chisi* was "a sacred day devoted to the spirits, during which agricultural work in the fields is prohibited" as a sign of respect to the relationship between the spirits and the land.[9] Since resting was configured in religious language, it was everyone's obligation. Disobeying *chisi* was considered detrimental to the productivity of land, women and cattle.

---

[7] Andrew D. Roberts and, Roland Anthony Oliver (eds), *The Cambridge History of Africa*, vol. 7, c. 1905—c. 1940 (Cambridge: Cambridge University Press, 1986), 123.

[8] David Lan, *Guns & Rain: Guerrillas & Spirit Mediums in Zimbabwe* (Berkeley: University of California Press, 1985), 92.

[9] Michael F. C. Bourdillon, *The Shona Peoples* (Harare: Mambo Press, 1987).

## Slavery, colonialism and the missionaries

Inevitably, the African traditional understanding was influenced by the contact
with other cultures. The impacts of slavery and colonialism were particularly
felt in terms of reshaping African conceptions of work. Even though slavery
did not directly affect the people of southern Africa as it did those from the
west and east, four hundred years of slavery changed the way in which Africans
were to understand work in general. It must be pointed out that tribal raids and
forced labor were not new phenomena, introduced by Europeans. Nonetheless,
while such scenarios existed before the arrival of the Europeans, they cannot
be compared to the systematic, widespread and large-scale operations that
took place when Africans encountered the new arrivals mainly from Europe.
Initially, these new neighbors were looking for gold and other minerals, as well
as ivory and other tradable goods. But once they saw opportunities for making
larger profits than had been initially imagined and spurred on by burgeoning
industries that required more labor, their imagination was stretched. They
seized the opportunity to buy slaves who could provide cheap labor in the
newly established "sugar factories" in the Caribbean, Latin America, etc. It
was mainly the Portuguese, the British, the French, the Spanish, the Dutch
and the North Americans, in this order of scale, who led the transatlantic slave
trade. From the fifteenth century onwards, this system was mainly operated
by Spanish and Portuguese traders and was then further expanded by other
Europeans towards the end of the sixteenth and beginning of the seventeenth
centuries.[10] In its heyday, the slave trade catchment area extended across 3,500
kilometers, from the mouth of the Senegal River to Angola, with almost 12
million slaves being shipped abroad. [11] This had a tremendous impact on how,
in the future, Africans were to perceive work.

First, if by selling human beings to these traders one could avoid toiling
on the land where production could be unpredictable, it would be preferable
to sell some few individuals and be assured of a ready income than to wait for
the unpredictable rain and the work of the diviner, who by now had proved to
be weaker than the sophisticated ammunition of the slave traders. Secondly,
since the slave traders demonstrated how to treat slaves inhumanly in order to
extract maximum production, inhumane treatment quickly became associated
with work, and soon stronger local tribes or groups raided fellow Africans and
used them as their own slaves. Third, there where it was not possible to own

---

[10] Mark Tauger, *Agriculture in World History* (New York: Routledge, 2011), 75.

[11] Luz María Martínez Montiel, "Our Third Root. On African Presence in American Populations," in
*Diogenes* 45 (179), September 1997, 165–85.

slaves, wages became a new reality. Previously no one had been paid cash for their work; barter was the common form of trade and the way in which one helped one's neighbor wherever needed. Fourth, due to the displacement of persons fleeing the slavery frontiers into the African interior, agricultural production in the coastal regions dropped significantly. This resulted in important economic changes in the coastal and interior regions.[12]

The slave trade was an extension of another factor that radically reshaped the Africans' understanding of work, namely the colonization of Africa. While many slave traders took their loot back home or to their industrial sites, the colonizers stayed and owned the places and the people of Africa. The colonial era saw the "production and evolution of a global economy and associated structures of power and knowledge, in which exploitation and reworking of difference was both a driving force and a product" on African ground.[13] The industrialization and commercialization of work meant that, in a number of areas, Africans would have to reshape and adapt many aspects of their thinking about work.

First, colonialism enforced new ideas about land and property ownership. While Africans were used to work on the land associated with the burial sites of their ancestors who were thought of as guarantors of productivity, the colonial governments would remove people from this land if they deemed it useful for commercial agriculture, for example. Being relocated would obviously disorient the African person and bring much unpredictability to their work practices. Second, working for someone with whom they did not share a reciprocal relationship was a new concept for Africans who were conscripted to work on commercial farms, in mines and factories. Third, for the first time, Africans had to work away from their homes. My father, who was working for the colonial government as a policeman, lost his job when he returned from having buried his father since he had taken more time off than allowed. Fourth, for the first time, many Africans had to endure supervision. In the traditional work environment one had worked for oneself or with one's neighbors. There was no supervisor; one took responsibility for one's own work. What made this worse was that, usually, the supervisor was younger, which is contrary to African culture where age meant everything.

These are just some of the factors contributing to many Africans resenting work. Work became associated with enslavement, punishment and wages. The

---

[12] Chrystal Stillings Smith, *The Changing Economy of Mt Kilimanjaro, Tanzania: Four Essays on the Modernization of Smallholder Agriculture* (Utrecht: Geografisch Instituut, Rijksuniversiteit Utrecht, 1980).

[13] Eric Sheppard et al (eds), *A World of Difference. Encountering and Contesting Development* (New York: The Guilford Press, 2009), 319.

colonial regimes interpreted this resentment as laziness; hence the common phrase, the "lazy African." They would claim that the African would "prefer to remain under nourished and diseased rather than expend a little more energy in cultivation and adopt new practices."[14] Missionaries who tried to be sympathetic to the Africans would normally be told:

> There are certain aspects of the position of Christian missions in Africa that differentiate their task from that of missions in many of the non-Christian areas of the world. Missions in Central Africa deal with backward races who are in a different cultural cycle from the peoples of Asia, Europe or America. The universal communalism of Bantu tribal life gave small room for individual progress. An aristocracy or leisure class was not evolved, nor feudal courts in which the arts or crafts could be encouraged. For these and other reasons it has come about that these peoples possess neither a culture, arts not handcrafts which attract the European. The Bantu have no written language, records or literature, either philosophical, historical or religious. Their rich oral tradition and a wealth of fable shed light upon their background. With the exception of the ruins of Great Zimbabwe and contemporary irrigation works in Southern Rhodesia, ruins which are by many attributed to foreign invaders, they possess no monuments nor enduring witness of material achievements. The African of the areas of this study stands before the modern world with empty hands and with little apparent contribution to offer to world culture.[15]

Africans were to be forced to adopt new "habits of industry," and to be weaned from their "capricious and spasmodic habit of work."[16] Most missionaries came to the defense of Africans for different reasons. This was one missionary's response:

> The native has also his home, his crops, and his plans for development. The demands on his time may not be constant but they are insistent. To leave his own plantation, perhaps at a critical time, for the benefit of someone else's plantation; to leave his house unthatched, his crops unreaped, his wife unguarded perhaps for months at a time, in return for cash he does not want on the "advice" of his

---

[14] *Tour Report* No.2, 1947, Zambia National Archives section 2/963, quoted in Ann Whitehead, "The 'Lazy Man' in African Agriculture," in Cecile Jackson (ed.), *Men at Work: Labour, Masculinities, Development* (London: Frank Cass, 2001), 23–52, here 25.

[15] Merle Davis, *Modern Industry and the African* (London: Frank Cass and Company Limited, 1933), 1.

[16] Colin Bundy, *The Rise and Fall of the South African Peasantry* (Berkeley: University of California Press, 1979), 138.

chief—which he dare not disregard—is not a prospect calculated to inspire loyalty to the government from which the advice emanates.[17]

Work seen from the perspective of force and not based on relationships created a negative image of work. In 1952, a pan-African journal evaluated the Westerners' attitude to work as follows:

> Europe seems to me to be a continent which organizes itself progressively in an immense "work machine" whose substance expands throughout the world with a force that Europe itself cannot control... The entire European personality is thus a work machine and only finds its certain joys in work, in the largest sense of the term.[18]

## Toward an African theology of work: Bishop S. Strandvik

While "missionary bashing" may be a hobby for some, I want to make clear that the facts at our disposal show that missionaries differed widely and that they operated in highly complex situations. First, they had to prepare Africans to deal with the irreversible reality of modernity mediated by the colonial system and governments over which they had no control, and which they had to be careful not to antagonize lest they be denied permission to operate in these countries. Second, they were foreigners and in most cases did not understand local constructions of reality, at least in their finer workings. Therefore, even where they were genuinely trying to be considerate to Africans, they sometimes found themselves misinterpreting and miscommunicating with their African congregants.

In an effort to bridge the gap between themselves and the locals, the missionaries and the colonial governments built schools to orient Africans to Western thinking. The Lutheran Swedish missionaries built schools in the Mberengwa, Gwanda and Beitbridge areas, areas stretching to the Midlands and Matebeleland-south of Zimbabwe.[19] This is my home area and home to many Zimbabwean Lutherans. For the colonial regimes this was an important

---

[17] This is reference to J. W. Arthur of the Church of Scotland Mission in Uganda, in Robert W. Strayer, *Making of Mission Communities in East Africa: Anglicans and Africans* (New York: New York Press, 1978), 108.

[18] Alioune Diop, *Présence Africaine*, 13 (1952)), quoted in Jackson, op. cit. (note 14), 24.

[19] First they bought a farm at Mnene in 1903 although they only established the mission centre there in 1908. To Mnene were added Masase (1920), Gwanda (1928), Musume (1932), Zezani (1932), Manama (1938) and Masingo (1932), in Tor Sellström, *Sweden and National Liberation in Southern Africa: Volume 1, Formation of a Popular Opinion 1950-1970* (Uppsala: Nordiska Africa institute, 1999), 314.

development because Africans educated in the Western sense of education would make Africans better workers.

> The first task of education is to raise the standard alike of character and efficiency of the bulk of the people, but provisions must be made for the training of those who are required to fill posts in the administrative and technical services, as well as those who as chiefs will occupy positions of exceptional trust and responsibility. As resources permit, the door of advancement, through higher education, in Africa must be increasingly opened for those who by character, ability and temperament show themselves fit to profit from such education.[20]

This education, even for African chiefs, was meant to prepare them to "maintain the needs of the colonial system"[21] and to be able to bring them to the awareness that they were meant to work in subordinate positions since their education was not sufficient enough for them to assume higher positions. This education was not only to provide the know-how for the new administrative work in the colonial government but also to instill the work ethic necessary for such positions. The responsibility for this ethical "transformation" fell into the domain of the missionaries who took Africans through catechetical education. It must be pointed out here that this was the education that prepared Africans for liberation.

The focus here is on the changing African conceptions of work and recognizes the contribution of the catechetical education by the missionaries. In his catechetical work, Bishop Sigfrid Strandvik (Evangelical Lutheran Church in Rhodesia, bishop until 1975), interprets the seventh commandment in a way that reflects how African Christians were taught to think about God and work. Strandvik's work is important because he mixes Western concepts of work with African cultural notions of work, which reflects how most Africans began to move on with their lives after the colonial era. Many Africans were no longer traditional in how they regarded work, nor could they be completely modern. It is this fine balancing act that is the context for a contemporary African theology of work.

Strandvik developed an African explanation of Martin Luther's catechism, *Nzira Youpenyu: Dudziro Yekatikasi Doko Ya Martin Luther* [The way of life: Explaining Martin Luther's Small Catechism].[22] This was an important work

---

[20] Decision made in 1923 by the British Advisory Committee of Education for Tropical Africa, in Toyin Falola, *Nationalism and the African Intellectuals* (New York: University of Rochester Press, 2001), 11.

[21] Ibid., 12.

[22] Sigfrid Strandvik, *Nzira Youpenyu: Dudziro Yekatikasi Doko Ya Martin Luther*, sixth edition (Bulawayo: Mutasa Printers, 1951).

in that it reflected the ambivalence regarding the colonial discourse on work combined with an African contextualization, characteristic of missionary theology. Following Luther, who always began with the prohibitions and then moved to positive injunctions, Strandvik interpreted these prohibitions and injunctions. Luther's rendition of the seventh commandment is, "You shall not to steal. What is this? Answer: We are to fear and love God, so that we neither take our neighbors' money or property nor acquire them by using shoddy merchandise or crooked deals, but instead help them to improve and protect their property and income."[23] Having described the first two prohibitions of this commandment, that is, the prohibition to take someone's wealth, corruption and fraud, he goes on to the third prohibition where he talks about laziness. Here he combines laziness with unfaithfulness in one's work. In a pictorial way, he shows two men, one sleeping next to a wheelbarrow while asking his workmate, who is sitting on a shovel, *Zuva richavira rini?* [When is the sun going to set?].[24] He concludes that "Some people do not think about their work, they only look at the time wondering when the sun will set. They waste time and receive money they have not really worked for."[25]

Up to this point, he seems to singing from the colonial hymnal intended to instill a tough work ethic among Africans, since he seems to have wage labor in mind. This, in the postcolonial discourse, would be seen as a typical example of how religion was used to overcome the Africans' disillusionment with wage labor. A new concept of time was introduced here according to which time can be stolen or wasted, concepts which were not so much foreign as differently conceived of in the African thinking at the time. Especially in the rural areas, time is not only a commodity but a tool for building relationships. Therefore, when two men, one sitting on a shovel and the other relaxing next to a wheelbarrow, are conversing, it is likely that they are not wondering when the sun is going to set as Strandvik thinks. Rather, they are doing what normal Africans do when they work: they are building relationships through conversation.

When Strandvik comes to the second section dealing with what the commandment positively instructs people to do, the concept of work changes radically. According to Strandvik, the seventh commandment instructs people to help one another so that their wealth may increase. His explanation here is that we need to be concerned that our neighbor's wealth is not endangered. "We must watch so that cattle, goats and sheep do not get into the fields and destroy the

---

[23] Robert Kolb and Timothy J. Wengert (eds), *The Book of Concord: The Confessions of the Evangelical Lutheran Church* (Minneapolis: Fortress Press, 2000), 353.

[24] Strandvik, op. cit. (note 22), 27.

[25] Ibid., 27.

crops. When you borrow a hoe or a bicycle or someone else's property, you must handle it as if it were yours until you return them."[26] We are also instructed to help our neighbor so that their wealth increases by helping them in their work.[27] He then makes the rather ambiguous claim that "*vakuru vanoziva nzira yokubetserana pamubato nedoro*" [the elders know how to help each other with work and home brewed beer].[28] This can be interpreted in two ways: first, that the elders know ways of helping each other with work by gathering neighbors, whom they serve with home brewed beer, or that the elders help each other with work and they also share in their beer drinking. I think the first translation is correct since it is a description of the *humwe* referred to above. Strandvik continues, "we must learn from them, and even surpass them by helping each other in every work. We must particularly help those who find it difficult to work themselves like the widows."[29] Here Strandvik taps into African practices, uses them as the basis for developing an African Lutheran theology of work and radically departs from the then predominant modern industrial thinking that dominated work in his colonial context.

Important observations can be made regarding this second section of the commandment. First, it is now completely situated in traditional rural society, where animals are looked after and where old people set an example for society. The first scenario reflects urban life: young people are presented as despondent wage laborers. Thus the boy steals a pump from a bicycle, the sales person defrauds customers, the two young men wallow in laziness and borrow money without returning it.[30] The whole section is situated in urban areas and reflects on the younger generation that is trying to make sense of how to live their lives as individuals with no community support, and for whom there appears to be no hope. This is contrary to rural life, where he sees hope, even with African culture forming the basis for a Christian work ethic. Second, while the first section of the seventh commandment seems to be dealing with individuals, the second section emphasizes the collective.[31] Here people help one another build collective wealth, and for this to be possible, they tap into their cultural resources. In this context, work is enjoyable and the results of work improve the quality of life. At this point the missionaries parted ways with the colonial discourse, which for them undermined African culture and

---

[26] Ibid., 28, section 1.

[27] Cf. ibid., section 2.1.

[28] Ibid., 28, section 2.2.

[29] Ibid.

[30] Ibid., 28, sections 1.1b.; 1.2; 1.3; 1.4.

[31] Ibid.

its potential contribution to a Christian work ethic. The colonial discourse promoting modernity's understanding of work was seen as a threat to Christian values and hence rejected. The missionaries recognized the potential in rural African culture for preserving the Christian theology of work.

Taking Strandvik's work as a point of departure, one could try to construct an African theology of work that takes into consideration contemporary African perspectives on work as they live within a modern global context while remaining connected to some aspects of African traditional thinking. When I worked in a sugar industry I had my first experience of how modernity, brought in by colonialism, did not destroy how Africans think about reality in general and work in particular, regardless of whether or not they had been educated in Western schools. For example, my Afrikaner manager used to get very upset when he saw African workers helping each other even though they had been assigned specific tasks. If they were forced to be at their work bench, they would shout to one another, telling stories and laughing. One would wonder if they were concentrating on their work. Tools were viewed as animate even in this modern workshop. It was known for example that you would not go into a sugar cane truck and sit at the driver's seat without prior permission from the driver. It was common to find ritual snuff under the seat of trucks and tractors. It was not uncommon to hear that someone had gone to the traditional healer, diviner, or prophet to seek strength for their work or to seek a promotion. Some of these people were university graduates. What kind of theology of work can be developed in the context of this religiously changed environment of work?

As we can see, work is still done in cooperation with others and with the spiritual world. Work, in other words, is done in community with other human beings and in community with the divine. The African communitarian view of reality was criticized for its lack of self-criticism, and this criticism should stand. A communitarian understanding of relationships does not necessarily mean egalitarianism. Nonetheless, a communitarian outlook is more amenable to the biblical God of work in both the Jewish and Christian testaments. This is a God, who in the community of the Trinity, creates by the invitation "Let us make humankind in our image" (Gen 1:26). If we take this to refer to the Triune God, then we immediately have a dimension of God's work in community. This is repeated by Jesus in John when he says, "My Father is still working, and I also am working" (Jn 5:17). Jesus does not work in isolation but in cooperation with the Father and the Spirit. "When the Spirit of truth comes, he will guide you into all the truth; for he will not speak on his own, but will speak whatever he hears, and he will declare to you the things that are to come" (Jn 16:13).

Second, community alone does not guarantee equity as was demonstrated by African women theologians for instance. While African theology emphasized community, this community excluded women. Further, constructions of community also excluded children and other people at the margins. Where community is not reflective and self-critical, it results in other societal ills such as nepotism, ethnicity, tribalism and racism. Community becomes exclusivist. The panacea for this exclusivist communitarian view of work is to take seriously the sacramental view of life, where all material things have life and divine life in them. This sense of God's presence in all things is attested to in those Scriptures that allude to the ever presence of God, even when God had rejected God's people for their rebellion and sin.

Working with the understanding that we are not working alone or working on simply dead objects would change the way in which we do work. The potential for all material reality to become animate or to be infused with life once in contact with human beings can be an important contribution to a theology of work. The assumption that all things are sacred and hence all material things have relative levels of sacredness has potential for a comprehensive theology of work. The view that all material things are penetrated with divine power makes all work a holy engagement. It challenges all workers to take seriously their own roles as participants in the continuing work of creation since God is at work in all things. If our work is in cooperation with God, then this means that we treat raw materials and our fellow workers with respect. If the ground we stand on is holy ground, then we take off our shoes everywhere; hence no work is simply about profiteering. "Whoever speaks must do so as one speaking the very words of God; whoever serves must do so with the strength that God supplies, so that God may be glorified in all things through Jesus Christ," so Peter tells us (1 Pet 4:11).

Third, there is an inherent weakness in the above understanding of work, When applied to leadership work, the sacralization of persons in leadership can easily lead to some sense of theocracy resulting in the abuse of power. Here, Strandvik advises us to be driven by the care and concern of the neighbor's welfare, to protect and increase their wealth. Using one's office in order to increase the neighbor's welfare and wealth is one of the most challenging theological understandings in the context of the today's profit driven economies that pit individuals against each other in order to maximize profits. Here the winner takes all and the loser is completely downtrodden. An African theology of work, to which the neighbor's welfare is central, takes away all the evils of unhealthy competition. It is a theology that is confident to answer when God asks, "Where is your brother Abel?" (Gen 4:9), or no one will say about us, "I am running away from my mistress Sarai" (Gen 16:8) like Hagar.

## Conclusion

The dominant language of economic growth for Africa should be punctuated by traditional African thinking because it resonates with the Word of God. Traditional African and biblical values, applicable to economic thinking, come out very strongly in this attempt at an African theology of work. The agrarian economy of biblical Israel resonates with agrarian Africa at many levels. The history of aggressive cultural encounters, where the local culture found new ways of surviving the onslaught, is evident in both cases. What separates the two is that the one is located in the distant past while the other is still trying to find ways of establishing itself. The religious character of the African conception of reality in general and work in particular, requires that any attempt at constructing a relevant theology of work take this into serious consideration. We are yet to see concerted efforts being made to make Africa's religious outlook and heritage the basis for its future development. Maybe it is an African theology of work that could make a small contribution in that direction.

# Luther's Theology of Work— The Basis of a Just Economy

## Tom Kleffmann

### Introduction

Before dealing with the question of the theological significance of work, we must first define what is meant by work. This term does not cover only salaried or wage-earning activities, but also work within the home and the family, as well as other unremunerated work. Next, the theological significance of the various professions needs to be investigated. And lastly, labor needs to be considered within its overall economic context. We need, therefore, to examine how the meaning of work and the significance of the various professions can help shape a just economy. In the context of the market economy, this refers in particular to fair remuneration for work and fair prices for the products of work. Is there a genuinely theological yardstick for justice equivalent to that for the concept of sin? "Sin" as a theological concept refers primarily to our (failed) relationship with God. Does economic justice have something to do with our relationship with God? It goes without saying that the meaning of work cannot be genuinely discussed without at the same time considering the market economy and trade, as well as the correlation between work and property.

Despite its elementary character, Luther's thinking on this complex question is not only surprisingly relevant to today, but also radical. This is one of the reasons—and not the least—why the question of justice needs to be reexamined. Of course, what follows is only a schematic outline, leaving the historical and bibliographical contexts aside.

### The meaning of work

God destined humankind for activity, work, and meaningful action. As the bird is born to fly, so is man born to work.[1] "Doing" is an integral part of human existence: "The being and nature of man cannot for an instant be without

---

[1] Cf. *WA* 1, 505, 19–21 (*Decem praecepta*, 1518) and Martin Luther, "Treatise on Good Works, 1520," in Helmut T. Lehmann (ed.), *Luther's Works*, vol. 44 (Philadelphia: Fortress Press, 1966), 108.

doing or not doing something, enduring or running away from something (for, as we see, life never ceases)"[2]—but only through faith in the knowledge that it is justified by grace is humanity liberated to grasp the divine sense of work.

Whether under circumstances of sin or not, good works flow from faith. Work, insofar as it corresponds to a relation to God determined by faith, is worship. It follows that working time need not as a matter of principle be separated from time spent in worship and in prayer—this is one of Luther's totally new insights. Of course, faith can be the belief that it is pleasing to God when a "man works at his trade," but also when he "walks, stands, eats, drinks, sleeps and does all kinds of works for the nourishment of his body or for the common welfare." [3] This does not mean that brute, mindless labor of any kind is worship of God. Rather, faith is awareness of meaning, and "no man is so heavily burdened with his work that he cannot, if the will is there, speak with God in his work."[4]

The meaning of the day of rest, this "bodily and spiritual pause from work" on Sunday, that we "put aside the work of our hands and rest from our labor so that we may gather in church," is accordingly relativized: This bodily rest "is a necessity ... for the sake of ... the working class so that they might come to [hear] the word of God." The "spiritual rest" intended in this commandment, however, does not negate activity *per se*, but rather means "much more—that we let God alone work in us and that in all our powers do we do nothing of our own."[5] "Spiritual rest," therefore, concerns the formation of a faith that accompanies all that is done or left undone and that, in contradiction with the rational principle of pursuing one's own advantage and one's own way, tells us that it is not "we who live, but Christ who lives" in us.[6]

Original sin does not fundamentally change the true meaning of work, namely, love of one's neighbor and the fact that God provides for our sustenance. However, some sinners actually fail to see this meaning and others misuse it—sinners are loathe to work and when so inclined, do so out of self-interest and for their own welfare. For the Christian, however, who is liberated in terms of the meaning of work but still inclined toward sin, work has an additional function: self-discipline. This is dealt with in Theses 20–22 of *The Freedom of a Christian*, 1520. Although human beings are already justified by faith before God and freed from sin, death and Satan, they must exercise their bodies by

---

[2] Luther, ibid., 34.

[3] Ibid., 24.

[4] Ibid., 61.

[5] Ibid., 72.

[6] Ibid., 73.

"fastings, watchings, labor, and other reasonable discipline ... and conform to the inner man" united with Christ in faith. Together with love of neighbor, this self-conformity is the main purpose of good works. Without this discipline, the flesh would succumb to the will that characterized the old self and which, in its relationship to others, seeks its own gratification. [7]

As already said, meaningful work is directed toward our neighbor's welfare, on the one hand, and to our own subsistence, on the other. Here, subsistence as the purpose of work needs to be distinguished from Mammon, that is, work for false gods or to acquire property through which a person defines themselves, instead of experiencing their true identity in the relationship with God and the corresponding love of neighbor.

In his work *Whether Soldiers, Too, Can Be Saved* (1526), Luther writes:

> It is not wrong to do things for temporal wealth ... If it were wrong, no one should work or do anything to support himself ... But to be greedy of temporal wealth and make a Mammon of it is always wrong in every office, position and occupation. [8]

With regard to work as a means of livelihood, another distinction needs to be made. Faith means working with the knowledge that God provides for me both bodily and spiritually. Our labors "in the fields, in the garden, in the city, in the house, in war, or in government" should be like a prayer that God bless this activity and bestow the corresponding fruits. God gives us the purpose of our work: "Labor, and let Him give the fruits. ... In all our doings He is to work through us, and He alone shall have the glory from it." [9]

God wants no lazy idlers. People should work diligently and faithfully according to their calling and profession and then God will give blessing and success.

Here we need to distinguish the thought of working to provide for oneself and relying on what one achieves by oneself. The point is, "don't rely solely on your own work and doings. Get busy and work, and yet expect everything from God alone." [10]

---

[7] Cf. Martin Luther, "The Freedom of a Christian, 1520," in Helmut T. Lehmann (ed.), *Luther's Works*, vol. 31 (Philadelphia: Muhlenberg Press, 1957), 358–59.

[8] Martin Luther, "Whether Soldiers, Too, Can Be Saved, 1526," in Helmut T. Lehmann (ed.), *Luther's Works*, vol. 46 (Philadelphia: Muhlenberg Press, 1967), 130.

[9] Martin Luther, "Psalm 147," in Jaroslav Pelican (ed.), *Luther's Works*, vol. 14 (St. Louis: Concordia Publishing House, 1958), 114.

[10] Ibid., 115

To be sure, a person should not expect a "roasted chicken to fly into his mouth." Nonetheless,

> he is not to be anxious, not covetous; he is not to despair that he is not going to have enough. … "As the bird is born to fly, so man is born to work." Now birds fly without anxiety and without covetousness, and so we should work without anxiety and without covetousness.[11]

Anxiety, like concupiscence, is a form of non-belief. Anxiety and the work of anxiety obey the pattern of the fundamental sin of the "old self" by which people live in and through themselves, and themselves mediate their identity in relation to the world.

Those who work out of greed or in such a way that they sink into total anxiety for themselves or whatever touches upon them, also miss the truth of a created, meaningful life. In truth, that person lives, with every breath, at every moment, on gifts that God bestows on all humankind. In contrast, the "sealed-off-ness" in which a person takes these gifts of life for granted is once again an expression of the inherited imprisonment of humankind within itself. This sealed-off-ness is realized not only in the motivation to work, but also through its success—the person defines themselves in relation to an artificial world of the fruits of their labor, thus becoming the creator of their world and identity. In his 1530 "Exposition of Psalm 118" Luther wrote:

> If we human beings were not so blind and so smug and indifferent toward the blessings of God, there would not be a man on earth, no matter how wealthy, who would trade an empire or a kingdom for them; for he would surely be robbed in the deal. What is a kingdom compared with a sound body? What is all the money and wealth in the world compared with one sunlit day? Were the sun to stop shining for one day, who would not rather be dead; for what would then be the value of wealth and power? What would the finest wine … in the world amount to if we had to go without water for one day? What would our magnificent castles, houses, silk, satin, purple, golden jewelry, precious stones, all our pomp and glitter and show help us if we had to do without air for the length of one Our Father?
>
> These gifts of God are the greatest and also the most despised. Because they are so common, no one thanks God for them. People simply accept and use them daily, as though it had to be so, and we had a perfect right to them and

---

[11] Luther, op. cit. (note 1), 108.

did not even need to thank God. In the meantime they are quick and frantic to do, worry, quarrel, wrangle, strive, and storm after unnecessary money and goods, honor and luxury—in short, after something which cannot hold a candle to the blessings mentioned above. These things are not worth a fraction of the others. Instead, they hinder us in the happy and peaceful enjoyment of the common blessings, so that we can neither recognize them as such nor thank God for them.[12]

Returning to the meaning of work, for Luther, one's own subsistence and love of neighbor are not excluded as the meaning [purpose] of work. Basing himself on the general division of work, Luther believes that, in principle, all work, even if it is for one's own benefit and is correspondingly motivated, still contributes to the common good—in the preindustrial economic system, Luther cites in particular those who have the responsibility of feeding (i.e., farmers) and those who have the responsibility of defending, that is, of preserving external peace. The separate, third estate, comprised of those who teach, is the clergy.[13] To the extent that all estates are of public utility, that is, they collectively serve the common good, all work is worship of God and service to others—and it is again faith that brings this about. The public utility of work deriving from the division of work, for Luther, is an order willed by God: God provides that "one always needs the other ... What would princes, nobles, and regents be if there were not others, such as pastors, preachers, teachers, farmers, craftsmen, etc.? They would not and could not learn or do everything alone and by themselves," Luther said in a sermon in 1544.[14]

Work, and the result of work, can be good and serve the common welfare whatever the office or profession even if its real, personal motivation is wrong and the work with regard to the "individual" is sin. "Work, in itself, is just and godly, but ... it becomes wrong if the person is unjust or uses it unjustly."[15]

We know that the German word *Beruf* meaning "profession" goes back to Luther. It is God who calls (*beruft*) to a specific type of work to serve the common good.[16] Consequently, for Luther, as Max Weber observed a century

---

[12] Luther, "Psalm 118," in op. cit. (note 9), 48–49.

[13] Cf. for example, op. cit. (note 8).

[14] Martin Luther, "Sermon at the Dedication of the Castle Church in Torgau, Luke 14:1–11, 1544," in Helmut Lehmann (ed.), *Luther's Works*, vol. 51 (Philadelphia: Muhlenberg Press, 159), 351–352.

[15] Luther, op. cit. (note 8), 130.

[16] Cf. Andreas Pawlas, *Die lutherische Berufs- und Wirtschaftsethik. Eine Einführung* (Neukirchen–Vluyn: Neukirchener, 2000); Max J. Suda, *Die Ethik Martin Luthers* (Göttingen: Vandenhoek & Ruprecht, 2006), 138ff.; Peter Mörbel and Otto Strecker (eds), *Beruf und Berufung. Der Stellenwert von Luthers Berufsethos in der globalisierten Wirtschaft* (Bonn: Evang. Akad, im Rheinland, 2009).

ago, every station and profession has equal value in the eyes of God.[17] It is obvious that this fact of being equal in value must then also be a basic criterion in relation to the question of justice, for example, with regard to wages. This will be discussed at more length later.

Clearly the common utility of work based on the division of labor also needs to be examined critically. Luther discusses this especially in relation to the case where the authority imposes military service, that is, the "work" of soldiers. In the case of an unjust war, for example a war of aggression or expansion, the soldier must refuse to "work."[18] Luther, however, is also critical with regard to the production of luxury goods and to trade. This will also be discussed further.

According to Luther, it is consistent with the natural and divine orders that one's means of livelihood, including the possessions that go with it, is earned through work. Conversely, income without work is an injustice; in fact, it is thieving from those who work. Here Luther places begging by monks and interest on capital and commercial profits gained through domination of the market on an equal footing. Seeking such forms of income is a direct expression of concupiscence, that is, the cupidity which characterizes fundamental or original sin. It is "usury-seeking greed ... or the Old Adam that does not like to work to earn its bread."[19]

According to Luther, it is incumbent upon the secular authority to combat this inclination and to oblige everyone to work.[20] In *To the Christian Nobility of the German Nation Concerning the Reform of the Christian Estate*, 1520, he writes:

> He who has chosen poverty ought not to be rich. If he wants to be rich, let him put his hand to the plow and seek his fortune from the land. It is enough if the poor are decently cared for so that they do not die of hunger or cold. It is not fitting that one man should live in idleness on another's labor, or be rich and live comfortably at the cost of another's hardship, as it is according to the present perverted custom. St. Paul says, "Whoever will not work shall not eat" [II Thess. 3:10]. God has not decreed that any man shall live off another

---

[17] Cf. also *WA* 28, 445, 11ff. (sermon John 20:1–10); *WA* 37, 275, 24ff. (sermon Matt 20:1ff.), 276, 16ff.; *WA* 49, 606, 20ff.; 608, 30; op. cit. (note 14), 350, "the maidservant has the same dignity as the noblest empress"); Max Weber, *Die Protestantische Ethik*, vol 1, ed. J. Winckelmann (Gütersloh: Siebenstern, 1978), 68.

[18] Cf. op. cit. (note 8), 130, para. 2.

[19] *WA* 6, 7, 12f. Martin Luther, "Trade and Usury, 1524," in Helmut T. Lehmann, *Luther's Works*, vol. 45 (Philadelphia: Muhlenberg Press, 1962, 306).

[20] "However, he [the prince] should not tolerate useless people, who ... live in idleness, and drive them out of the land, as do the bees, which sting the drones to death because they do not work." Op. cit. (note 8), 128.

man's property, save only the clergy who preach and have a parish to care for, and these should, as St. Paul says in I Corinthians 9[:14], on account of their spiritual labor.[21]

Basically, this also addresses the problem of income derived from trade and capital. Of course, even when property seems to be inequitably distributed and "one may lie idle thanks to the work of others," the legal protection of property—the prohibition of stealing and theft—is necessary. In general, when in conflict, the preservation of the rule of law takes precedence over equitable distribution. For Luther, in the case of a breakdown of the legal order, the general tendency even within Christianity to take advantage of others that continues to exist in the Christian world would be exacerbated. Theologically speaking, reliance on self justice in relation to the questions of just and unjust possession is thus to be rejected—Luther exposed this principle in the case of the Peasants' War of 1525 in particular. In the *Admonition to Peace a Reply to the Twelve Articles of the Peasants in Swabia, 1525*, he wrote:

> Dear friend, the gospel does not teach us to rob or to take things, even though the owner of the property abuses it by using it against God, wrongfully, and to your injury. ... appropriate the tithe ... That is the same as deposing the rulers altogether.[22]

Of course, Christians should be so free as to renounce their possessions as mentioned in the Sermon on the Mount. This, however, does not call into question the necessity of the legal protection of property.

## The problem of the dissociation of trade and the market economy from the hermeneutical context of labor. What is a just price?

Luther is critical of trade. The question is whether it is subsumed under work as serving the common good by, for example, organizing the distribution of products. Only in this way is it justifiable and not an expression of concupiscence. Accordingly, income from trade must be understood as wages for work.

---

[21] Martin Luther, "To the Christian Nobility of the German Nation Concerning the Reform of the Christian Estate, 1520," in op. cit. (note 1), 190–91. Cf. 2 Thess 3:10.

[22] Op. cit. (note 8), 37–38.

On the other hand, the unchecked dissociation of trade from work as well as the enjoyment of its fruits may be driven by the personal greed of merchants. The justification of this development in the relatively general greed of consumers, which is an expression of the persistence of fundamental or original sin, is at least as significant.

For Luther, it is the general desire for goods in excess of what is needed for subsistence and that serve as surrogate gods, that makes global trade necessary as opposed to the regional distribution of regional products. The resultant dissociation of trade from work and from the necessity of a regional exchange of goods, as well as the separation of money from its pragmatic role as a medium is once again, exacerbated and increased by the dissociation between the financial industry—that is, the money trade—and material trade. This leads to the unjustified amassing of wealth without actual work.

The following passage from the *To the Christian Nobility of the German Nation Concerning the Reform of the Christian Estate*, 1520 illustrates this:

> By the grace of God more things to eat and drink grow in our own land than in any other, and they are just as nourishing and good. Perhaps my proposals seem foolish, impractical, and give the impression that I want to ruin the greatest of all trades, that of commerce. [...]
>
> But the greatest misfortune of the German nation is certainly the zynskauf If that did not exist many a man would have to leave his silks, velvets, golden ornaments, spices, and display of every kind unbought. This traffic has not existed much longer than a hundred years, and it has already brought almost all princes, endowed institutions, cities, nobles, and their heirs to poverty, misery, and ruin. [...]
>
> In this connection, we must put a bit in the mouth of the Fuggers and similar companies. How is it possible in the lifetime of one man to accumulate such great possessions, worthy of a king, legally and according to God's will?[23]

Similarly, in *Trade and Usury*, 1524, Luther called on the authorities to limit the self-regulation of the financial industry, especially as regards the lending of funds for the purposes of speculation. This suggests that the self-regulation of the financial industry could lead to economic collapse if the sums speculated are not covered by a minimum of equity.[24]

---

[23] Op. cit. (note 21), 212–13,

[24] Cf., op. cit. (note 19), 260, "That is why everyone now wants to be a merchant and get rich. From this stem the countless dangerous and wicked devices and dirty tricks that have today become a joke among the merchants. There are so many of them that I have given up the hope that trade can be entirely cor-

More importantly, however, the further the self-regulation of trade progresses, the more the fundamental ethical issue is blurred. The fundamental ethical issue can be expressed in terms of just price. Due to the fact that individuals are generally greedy, there is a tendency to take advantage of others and to take from them unlawfully. That is, merchants seek a price that is not justified in terms of work or performance. They seek a profit that is made possible by a scarcity of the goods on the market. This profit, therefore, is founded in the power of the owner over those who need the goods. The following principle applies: "I may sell my goods as dear as I can"; for Luther, this means "I care nothing about my neighbor."[25]

A just price is one that is based solely on the value of the goods, calculated according to total work and the cost of insurance against trade risks. In case of doubt, the secular authority should check the greed of the market and set the prices. One could say, rather anachronistically, that Luther wanted to integrate powerful planning elements into the market economy in order to give the market economy a social justice-oriented framework.

> But in order not to leave the question entirely unanswered, the best and safest way would be to have the temporal authorities appoint in this matter wise and honest men to compute the costs of all sorts of wares and accordingly set prices which would enable the merchant to get along and provide for him an adequate living, as is being done at certain places with respect to wine, fish, bread, and the like. But we Germans have too many other things to do; we are too busy drinking and dancing to provide for rules and regulations of this sort. Since this kind of ordinance therefore is not to be expected, the next best thing is to let goods be valued at the price for which they are bought and sold in the common market, or in the land generally. [...]
>
> Where the price of goods is not fixed either by law or custom, and you must fix it yourself, here one can truly give you no instructions but only lay it on your conscience to be careful not to overcharge your neighbor, and to seek a modest living, not the goals of greed. [...] Therefore, you must make up your mind to seek in your trading only an adequate living. Accordingly, you should compute and count your costs, trouble, labor, and risk, and on that basis raise or lower the prices of your wares so that you set them where you will be repaid for your trouble and labor[26]

---

rected; it is so overburdened with all sorts of wickedness and deception that in the long run it will not be able to sustain itself, but will have to collapse inwardly of its own weight."

[25] Ibid., 247, Luther called this the "chief maxim and rule of the whole business."

[26] Ibid., 249–50.

Should the authority fail to guarantee socially just prices, the merchant must take the long-term, common market price as the reference. It is hoped that market practice will ensure more or less appropriate prices. This, however, presupposes either that the power of the players (buyers and sellers) is not too unequal, in order to maintain the mutual dependence of the players, or that the social and ethical ties between players of regional markets (local customs) ensure a relatively just balance. If this principle cannot be applied, the owner and the merchant must let their consciences be their guide when setting prices according to "costs, trouble, labor and risk" and determine the fair trade benefit on that basis.

For the calculation of a just price, including the appropriate trade profits, Luther applies the principle of the "equivalent value of all work." If, in order to determine the just price of the goods, the merchant reckons the time worked, the measure to be used should be a day laborer's normal wage.

> In determining how much profit you ought to take on your business and your labor, there is no better way to reckon it than by computing the amount of time and labor you have put into it and comparing that with the effort of a day laborer who works at some other occupation ... .[27]

The proper measure, therefore, is the amount of God-given time that a person devotes to work. Should merchants quote a higher value for their work, it is to be assumed that once again, they are acting out of personal greed that leads them to abuse their *de facto* power over their neighbor.[28]

However, what Luther's critique does not include is the distinction between the absolute (i.e., essential to life) and relative scarcity of a certain merchandise on the market. The adaptation of the price according to supply and demand, therefore, seems acceptable as a means of regulating potential overproduction. With regard to the supply of goods over and above what is necessary to the subsistence of everyone (and only relatively scarce), adapting the price to supply and demand is justified. To what extent that is compatible with the principle of the equivalent value of time worked need not be further discussed here.

What, in Luther's view, are the criteria for justice with regard to income and prices? I identify two such criteria. First: Income corresponding to performance is just, whereas profit without corresponding work or performance (which includes, for example, insurance against risk) is theft or robbery against

---

[27] Ibid., 251.

[28] Even differences of remuneration to wage earners are subject to criticism to the extent that they are justified merely on the basis of a difference in the market value of their work.

those who work.[29] The first criterion, therefore, is the command to earn one's living through work, on the one hand and, on the other, God's command not to steal. The underlying principle is that the value of a person's time, or more specifically, a person's time worked, is not determined by the market; rather, ethically and in the eyes of God, it is of equal value [for all].

The second criterion of justice is another divine, Christian commandment to love one's neighbor: in the market also I am to "care about my neighbor." Therefore, provided a person is willing to work but cannot earn enough to guarantee their subsistence, that person's need is a criterion for Christian action. Of course, it remains to be determined theologically what, or which spirit, can liberate human beings to fulfill this commandment.

## The ways owners abuse their power in the market

Luther's criteria for judging the economic system of his time are as simple as they are radical. The brilliant sociologist Max Weber, in contrast to Calvin, attributed to him a kindly unworldliness. Many, still today relevant, examples of the way in which Luther critiqued the abuse of power by the owners on the market show that Luther was not uninformed with regard to the interrelatedness of work, trade, capital, prices, wages, etc. Quite the contrary, they show that he was keenly aware of the real phenomena of the nascent capitalistic market economy. I will give four such examples.

There is a central mechanism that is responsible for the decoupling of the market price from the factors of production including labor, indeed, the decoupling of the market price from its theologically just value. This concerns the aforementioned link between price and scarcity. Luther criticizes thus:

> Again there are some who sell their goods at a higher price than they command in the common market, or than is customary in the trade; they raise the price of their wares for no other reason than because they know that there is no more of that commodity in the country, or that the supply will shortly be exhausted, and people must have it. That is the rogue's eye of greed, which sees only the neighbor's need; not to relieve it, but to make the most of it and get rich at his expense. All such fellows are manifest thieves, robbers, and usurers.[30]

---

[29] This is particularly the case with regard to the lending of capital on interest. Concerning the idea that usury, which is the term one tended to use at the time to refer mainly to the charging of interest, is to be understood as robbery of the worker who produced work of an equivalent value. Cf. already in the "Short Sermon on Usury, 1519," *WA* 6, 7,7ff.; 8,22ff., as reproduced in op. cit. (note 19), 306ff.

[30] Op. cit. (note 19), 262.

A specific example of abuse of the free market economy criticized by Luther concerned price dumping for the purpose of constituting a monopoly. According to Luther, the corresponding stratagem is thievery and extortion. He firmly calls for regulation on the part of the secular authority, including the possibility of dispossession.

> Some of them, when they see that they cannot otherwise effect their selfish profiteering transactions and establish their monopolies because others have the same goods and wares, proceed to sell their goods so dirt cheap that the others cannot meet the competition, and are forced either to withhold their goods from sale, or to face ruin by selling them as cheaply as their competitors do. Thus, the greedy ones get their monopoly after all. Such fellows are not worthy to be called human beings or to live among men; they are not even worth admonishing or instructing, for their envy and greed is so open and shameless that even at the cost of their own losses they cause loss to others, in order that they may have the whole place to themselves. The temporal authorities would do right if they took from such fellows everything they had, and drove them out of the country.[31]

He criticizes just as firmly the stratagem of artificial shortages and cartelization. In this case too, the authorities must curtail the freedom of the market insofar as it is merely a freedom of greed on the part of owners of capital to exercise a usurped, God-like freedom and power over others that supersede all natural and Christian obligation toward the community.

> Here is another piece of selfish profiteering: Three or four merchants have in their control one or two kinds of goods which others do not have, or do not have for sale. When these men see that the goods are valuable and are advancing in price all the time because of war or some disaster, they join forces and let it be known to others that the goods are much in demand, and that not many have them for sale. If they find any who have these goods for sale, they set up a dummy to buy up all such goods. When they have cornered the supply, they draw up an agreement to this effect: since there are no more of these goods to be had, we will hold them at such and such a price, and whoever sells cheaper shall forfeit so and so much.[32]

---

[31] Ibid., 264–65.

[32] Ibid., 266,

So they,

> oppress and ruin all the small businessmen, like the pike the little fish in the water, just as if they were lords over God's creatures and immune from all the laws of faith and love. [...]
>
> Kings and princes ought to look into this matter and forbid them by strict laws. But I hear that they have a finger in it themselves, and the saying of Isaiah [1:23] is fulfilled, "Your princes have become companions of thieves." They hang thieves who have stolen a gulden or half a gulden, but do business with those who rob the whole world and steal more than all the rest, so that the proverb remains true, "Big thieves hang little thieves."[33]

Since representatives of the secular authority tend to be subject to the same sin of greed, the secular legal order is prone to corruption and consequently strays from its role, willed by God, to curtail the consequences of sin. Here, Luther evokes, for example, the entanglement of princes in the global financial empire of the Fuggers. Yet, the problem of corruption is not a problem of the secular legal order *per se*, but rather a problem of its enforcement. Even when not only persons, but also structures of authority are corrupt, this merely makes the task of setting up a just secular authority more acute without calling it entirely into question.

This problem cannot readily be solved without the separation of powers. Luther thus held the apocalyptic hope and expectation that "princes and merchants, one thief with the other, he [God] will melt together ... as when a city burns to the ground, so that there shall be neither princes nor merchants any more. That time, I fear, is already at the door."[34] We continue to be committed to the democratic and social rule of law and mandate, to make use of the freedom that it guarantees and to strive—politically at least—for justice. The theological perspective on the sense of work, on justice in the area of wages and market justice appears as intemporal today as it did in Luther's day and age.

---

[33] Ibid, 270, 271–72.

[34] Ibid., 272.

# Luther, Marx and German Steel: Post-Reformation Reflections on Labor from a German Context

### Martin Robra

## Three entry points

Albeit centuries apart, both Martin Luther and Karl Marx have their roots in the German context. In many ways still a child of the premodern feudal world, Martin Luther witnessed the dawning of a new era: the growing importance of long distance trade, the rapid development of banks and financial instruments, the concentration of economic power in huge companies controlling production, trade and financial flows such as the Fugger and Welser, which Luther called *monopolia*. In *Trade and Usury* (1524), Luther critiques in detail the economic and financial practices of his day and reaches the following, challenging conclusion:

> My only advice is this: Get out; they will not change. If the trading companies are to stay, right and honesty must perish; if right and honesty are to stay, the trading companies must perish.[1]

Luther failed to stem the tide of the emerging modern economic system, often referred to as capitalism, because of the new role and function of money and the financial system. Nonetheless, his core teachings on justification by grace and the distinction between gospel and law profoundly changed the understanding of vocation from a narrow medieval focus on contemplative and monastic life to the recognition that all forms of labor—including the manual labor of peasants and workers—are in the service of the community.[2]

---

[1] Martin Luther, "Trade and Usury, 1524," in Helmut T. Lehmann (ed.), *Luther's Works*, vol. 45 (Philadelphia: Muhlenberg Press, 1962), 272.

[2] Gustaf Wingren, *Luther on Vocation* (Philadelphia: Muhlenberg, 1957). Cf. Marc Kolden, "Luther on Vocation," in *Word and World* 3/4 (1983), 383–91.

Born 330 years after Luther, Karl Marx was confronted with the far-reaching transformation of societies as a consequence of the introduction of the steam engine and other new technologies. The disparities between labor and capital and the marginalization of the poor and dispossessed became apparent in the rapidly changing industrializing societies of the nineteenth century. Karl Marx devoted his entire life to analyzing the situation and to supporting the impoverished masses in their struggle against those in power. He had a formative influence on the Communist and socialist parties and trade unions, struggling for the right to work and decent wages.

Starting my service with my church in a congregation of steel workers south of Bochum in Germany, the postal address of the church was Karl Marx Street 23, with Friedrich Engels and Rosa Luxemburg Street just around the corner—all this during the Cold War in the Federal Republic of Germany. Old steel workers in the congregation would remember reading books by Marx and Engels (*Das Kapital* or *Anti-Dühring*) on the factory floor before the Nazis imprisoned and murdered the Communist and social-democratic leadership in the concentration camps. Those who had survived had their own interpretation of the story of Christ and the gospel, which came very close to the sociohistorical exegesis that was developed at the same time.[3] Reading the Bible together with steel workers, who had fought against the closure of their steel plant, taught me a lot.

One of the lessons we had to learn together was that the closure of the furnaces and the rolling mills was a result of the German steel companies' more recent strategies of "global outsourcing" and "international division of labor." For instance, German steel production shifted to Brazil in search for higher profits. From the mid seventies onwards, the reality of the increasing number of transnational corporations was discussed by the World Council of Churches (WCC) and by social and political scientists.[4] Later this process of change was to be called globalization.[5]

---

[3] Sociohistorical criticism (exegesis) was promoted in Germany by biblical scholars such as Luise Schottroff, Wolfgang Stegemann, Frank Crüsemann, Gerd Theissen, in the USA by Norman K. Gottwald and others together with contextual approaches.

[4] Cf. the study on transnational corporations by the Commission on the Churches' Participation in Development (CCPD) Advisory Group on Economic Matters of the World Council of Churches and the studies of the Starnberg Institute published by Folker Fröbel, Jürgen Heinrichs, Otto Kreye, *Die neue internationale Arbeitsteilung*, at **http://library.fes.de/gmh/main/pdf-files/gmh/1978/1978-01-a-041.pdf**.

[5] Over the last three decades, there have been only three publications on labor related concerns by the WCC: CCPD Advisory Group on Economic Matters, *Labour, Employment and Unemployment. An Ecumenical Reappraisal* (Geneva: WCC, 1985); "Work in a Sustainable Society," in *The Ecumenical Review* 48/3 (Geneva: WCC, 1996); in cooperation with the International Labour Office, Dominique Peccoud (ed.), *Philosophical and Spiritual Perspectives on Decent Work* (Geneva: ILO, 2004). In 1996, Lukas Vischer published theological reflections on "labor in crisis" which include very helpful summaries of the earlier

Luther, Marx and German steel—this title stands for three perspectives, three entry points for reflections on labor that marked my formation as a young theologian from the Lutheran tradition in Germany. Every one of these three perspectives has its own integrity and cannot be subsumed to the other. And this not simply because they are rooted in different moments of history. It would be utterly inappropriate to "baptize" Karl Marx and claim him for the churches or a church tradition. He represents a critical voice which the churches should have listened to instead of letting themselves be used by the German emperor in his fight against the Communists and social democrats. One of the churches in which I served as a pastor was built in the late nineteenth century with money donated by the Empress Augusta Victoria. She signed the Bible for the altar referring to Luke 19:10, "For the Son of Man came to seek out and to save the lost." Ironically, both the biblical text and the empress were looking toward the marginalized and excluded, but from very different starting points and with very different outcomes in mind.

## Work in the service of the neighbor and the community

In many different cultures there was and continues to be a tendency to denigrate manual labor.[6] The medieval church was heavily influenced by the Greek and Roman traditions, where manual labor was first and foremost the task of slaves or simple farmers. By questioning the exclusive emphasis on contemplation and monastic life and underlining the importance of manual labor in the service of the neighbor and the community, Luther opened a new chapter. However, his is not a secularized perspective with a simple, optimistic perspective on the capacity of human beings to shape the world. He maintains a balance between the perspective on labor under the conditions of sin as hard work, toil and burden, and labor as a meaningful activity that contributes to the common good. Justified by grace and not by works, a Christian responds freely to God's grace for the best of the community.[7]

---

discussion in the ecumenical movement, the Roman Catholic social teaching, insights from the early church and Reformation, and biblical references to the discussion. Lukas Vischer, *Arbeit in der Krise* (Neukirchen-Vluyn: Neukirchener Verlag, 1996).

[6] Cf. Ali Khan, "The Dignity of Manual Labor," in *Columbia Human Rights Review* (2001), at **http://papers.ssrn.com/sol3/cf_dev/AbsByAuth.cfm?per_id=56125**; for the following, see Ali Khan's critique of Aristotle.

[7] Cf. Marc Kolden, op. cit. (note 2), who reflects on vocation in the context of creation and redemption (388 ff.) and of the distinction between gospel and law—indeed both uses of the law.

Luther stood at the crossroads. The fact that his context was a predominantly feudal society motivated his devastating judgment of the peasants' uprising. At the same time, he observed and responded to the trends that ushered in the new era of modernity. At times, this has been overlooked and Luther's writings were either used to defend a stratified model of society in the interest of the ruling élite, or to portray him as a herald of modernity and a secularized understanding of the economic and political spheres of society.

Something similar can be said about Jean Calvin. The Swiss theologian André Biéler has rescued Calvin from many of his modern interpreters, including the famous Max Weber.[8] Another Swiss theologian and ecumenist, Lukas Vischer, has nicely summarized the teachings of both Martin Luther and Jean Calvin in a German booklet with the title *Labor in Crisis*.[9] Vischer focuses on the Sabbath commandment as the key to Calvin's understanding of labor. God created the human being to water the gardens. Labor was an essential dimension of human life also before the fall. But everything finds its fulfillment in the celebration of the Sabbath day and in the renewal of the relationship with God. The role of labor is limited. All of that which is essential to life remains God's gracious and grace filled gift. In this sense also the fruits of labor remain God's gift. This was later interpreted as meaning that material wealth would be a visible sign of God's grace. Calvin, however, warned against too strong an emphasis on profit and wealth. He insisted on the necessity of labor for the best of the community and as a matter of just relationships. Labor merits just remuneration, but making profit is not its goal.

Both Martin Luther and Jean Calvin contributed to opening the doors to future developments regarding the restoration of the value of manual labor. This, in part, prepared the way for both: a secularized understanding of labor as one of the productive resources of the economic system together with land and capital, as well as the claim to just relationships between workers and entrepreneurs. Actually, the Roman Catholic Church has been less ambiguous regarding the essential role of labor and the need for just working conditions than many of the Protestant churches, which have more readily adjusted to

---

[8] Edward Dommen is well placed to say more about Jean Calvin; he has published a number of articles on Jean Calvin's economic and social teaching and edited the English version of André Biéler's groundbraking book: *Calvin's Economic and Social Thought* (Geneva: World Alliance of Reformed Churches, 2005); it is clear today that Max Weber's famous essay, *The Protestant Ethic and the Spirit of Capitalism* (published in German in 1904/1905, in English in 1930 and now available on the web at **http://xroads.virginia.edu/~HYPER/WEBER/toc.html**) captures only certain aspects of the picture, regarding Luther and Calvin and the development of capitalism.

[9] Vischer, op. cit. (note 5), 48–67.

the development of modern society, where labor was increasingly seen merely as a means to acquire property and the good life (John Locke).

## The value of human labor

In post-World War II Germany, the pastors who had formed fraternities in the Confessing Church during the time of fascism signed a declaration in 1947 in Darmstadt that had been drafted by the famous Swiss theologian Karl Barth. Compared to the Stuttgart declaration of guilt of 1945, this statement goes one, important step further. It names the anti-socialist bias of the church as one of the main reasons why the church became an ally of those right-wing forces in society that supported Hitler. The church should have listened more to the cry of the poor and should have taken the critique of Karl Marx and others more seriously.[10]

Concentrating on the material basis of all economic activity, Marx high-lighted the central role of labor, which is not only the source of all economic wealth in transforming natural resources into goods to satisfy human needs, but also contributes to the development of human beings and their changing social organization. Since labor is at the origin of human society, Marx strongly criticized the exploitation of workers by the rich factory owners, who appropri-ate the surplus value, and the alienation of workers from their products under the conditions of industrial production. Even worse, labor itself has become a commodity and people have to compete on the "labor market" in order to make their living or merely to survive. This has become a decisive disadvan-tage for the working class that is forced into competing with itself. According to Marx's analysis of the situation, a centre piece of such an unjust economic order is the concentration and centralization of the means of production in the hands of those who have access to the necessary capital. In order to liberate the creative forces of human beings, this has to be changed.

Luther and Calvin had restored the value of manual labor and, according to Marx's theory, labor becomes a basic anthropological characteristic of human life and human community. Over the last century, the extent to which Marx's class analysis has prepared the way for the denial of freedom and subjectivity (following the Russian Revolution), and has alienated workers from the churches

---

[10] For a thought-provoking and inspiring analysis of Karl Marx's understanding of labor and its relevance for theology, see Miroslav Volf, *Zukunft der Arbeit—Arbeit der Zukunft. Der Arbeitsbegriff bei Karl Marx und seine theologische Wertung* (München/Mainz: Christian Kaiser, 1988); in English, *Work in the Spirit. Toward a Theology of Work* (New York: Oxford University Press, 1991).

and blocked non-violent options for change, has frequently been discussed in Marxist–Christian dialogues.

When we were struggling against the closure of the steel plant in the Ruhr region, we clearly saw that the relationship between land, labor and capital continued to be skewed in favor of capital. We were hoping that the churches would move forward ecumenically in building on the prevalence of labor over capital, which is enshrined in the social teaching of the Roman Catholic Church. At the local level the cooperation with the Roman Catholic diocese was excellent but, all in all, the support from politicians and the church leadership was limited to friendly rhetoric. At the decisive moments they were afraid of conflict.

# Theology of Work, Opportunities and Challenges

## Pierre Martinot-Lagarde[1]

Can theologians, trade unionists, employers and governments meet and have a conversation on decent work? In many ways, this question appears somewhat peculiar, even surreal. Modernity has separated the realms and we are accustomed to separating the religious sphere from other domains of public life. During the recent financial and economic crises, churches have drawn attention to the disastrous effects the turmoil was expected to have, and indeed has had, in terms of employment, social protection and respect for labor rights. In so doing, the churches were acting in concert with other political bodies at the national and international levels. Dialogues between religious and political bodies were organized, but while churches invited experts and politicians to join the voices of religious leaders, few religious leaders were invited to public institutions in order to share their views, invite to change or point to the necessity to respect the fundamental aspects of human dignity. This was probably not due to "bad will" or "bad intentions," but rather reflects important divisions between church and state.

## Convergences between the decent work agenda and Christian traditions

The ILO's Decent Work Agenda[2] is constructed around four, corresponding pillars. According to the ILO Declaration on Social Justice for a Fair Globalization, adopted in 2008, these pillars are interactive and mutually supportive.[3] They can be used as the starting point for examining convergences with Christian theology. In this area, the principal domains of interaction are a theology of creation, the relationship between God and human beings in this world, and a theology of redemption, the way in which God's and human beings' actions

---

[1] Pierre Martinot-Lagarde is special advisor for socioreligious affairs at the International Labour Organisation (ILO). The ideas expressed here reflect solely the views of the author and not those of the ILO.

[2] At **www.ilo.org/global/about-the-ilo/decent-work-agenda/lang--en/index.htm.**

[3] At **www.ilo.org/wcmsp5/groups/public/@dgreports/@cabinet/documents/publication/wcms_099766.pdf.**

collaborate. Finally, we could say that Christology—as Christ becoming the measure, model and the horizon of Christian life—is also a fundamental element. These fundamental aspects of Christian theology will influence our discussion on the decent work agenda and this essay is constructed around the following four pillars.

(i)    promoting employment by creating a sustainable institutional and economic environment ...

(ii)   developing and enhancing measures of social protection—social security and labour protection—which are sustainable and adapted to national circumstances ...

(iii)  promoting social dialogue and tripartism ...

(iv)   respecting, promoting and realizing the fundamental principles and rights at work, which are of particular significance, as both rights and enabling conditions that are necessary for the full realization of all of the strategic objectives ...[4]

Each one of these pillars touches on fundamental theological and anthropological questions. The pursuit of employment initiatives reflects on the meaning of work and its significance for human life in the context of creation. The notion of social protection has two dimensions: the objective of protection and security and solidarity as a way of pursuing this objective. The third pillar refers to the nation in the context of labor. The last pillar relates to the notion of human dignity as essential with regard to the respect and implementation of rights that are not merely there to protect but also to enable.

The notion of employment invites us to reflect on how work is interpreted in the Christian tradition, where work is perceived both as a positive and a negative notion. Work is the way in which humankind is associated with God's creation. It is also the way in which humankind found its own place after the expulsion from the Garden of Eden. Jesus is portrayed as the son of a carpenter. In the Bible, various trades and professions are portrayed positively such as the pastor and the fisher. Paul, for instance, did not beg but made a living from his work as a tentmaker. While sometimes work is associated with suffering, certain conditions of suffering and exploitation are clearly to be avoided, such as the enslavement of the Jews in Egypt, a situation which prevented them from revering God. While Matthew's trade as a publican is viewed negatively, it did not prevent Matthew from following Christ. Soon after the resurrection, the apostles return to their respective trades. Work is

---

[4] Ibid.

very much part of the "ordinary condition" of humankind; being deprived of work has serious consequences.

Security and protection are often combined and the second pillar of the Decent Work Agenda accomplishes exactly that. In the Christian tradition, a common source of reflection is the parable of the Good Samaritan. Here the old professions do not live up to their reputation. Neither the priest nor the Levite stops to help the man whose life has been threatened by robbers. Rather, it is the foreigner who felt called to act, providing security and protection and restoring the chain of solidarity. Securing basic needs appears to be one way of accomplishing salvation. Matthew 25 and John 6 are very explicit here. Security and food do not come out of nowhere, but are the result of the contribution of the one who has something to contribute.

The third pillar, the option for social dialogue in order to make the necessary adjustments in the world of labor, is directly derived from the industrial context. Adequate solutions are best found when governments, employers and workers come together to negotiate. Dialogue is preferable to open conflict and provides better solutions. In practice, dialogue and social dialogue mean bringing to the table parties with different, and often conflicting, interests in order to negotiate a compromise acceptable to all parties. The gospel does not provide an example of such a settlement. Rather, when Jesus was asked to settle a dispute about inheritance—a conflict that entailed what would appear to be irreconcilable differences—Jesus did not want to enter into the discussion. Nonetheless, the gospel refers to numerous conflicts, for example, between Jesus and his parents; lawyers, judges and ordinary people; the rich and the poor. The adulterous woman is a good example of where Jesus constructs a space for dialogue. Everyone in the crowd holds a stone, ready to lapidate the woman. One by one they reflect on their lives and leave the scene. In some cases, Jesus is the loser, as, for instance, in the case of the woman who compares herself to a dog and accepts to take the scraps left on the table. Jesus' trial, as reported by John, is a masterpiece of constructed dialogue in an open environment of conflict. Those who, in the first place, appear to be the winners, the Jews, are betrayed by Pilate. If Jesus is condemned, it is not because he said "he was the king of the Jews," it is because "he is the king of the Jews." *Quod scripsi scripsi*

The fourth pillar relates to fundamental rights at work and is centered on the notion of human dignity. The fundamental rights—no forced labor; the eradication of the worst forms of child labor; freedom of association; collective bargaining; no discrimination—are considered as enabling, meaning that they provide the basis for social improvement. Forced labor can be associated with slavery, but also with liberation. The story of Exodus speaks of the value of freedom. The freeing of the

Israelites from the domination of the Egyptians and the pharaoh marks the beginning of a long story and opens up the path to a process of liberation. They cannot be the people of Yahweh and revere God in slavery. The gospel tells us little about the conditions of children. However, forcing children to work in inhumane conditions not only deprives them of their personal future, but the whole of society of its future. Freedom of association is central to the way in which we understand faith. Creating human bonds is not an option, but it is central to our lives. The question of discrimination in the world of work arises here. The fundamental rights at work refer to the 1958 C 111 Discrimination (Employment and Occupation) Convention,[5] which states that in employment and all other related topics (training, access to benefit), there should be no discrimination based on race, sex or creed. It would be hard to find a direct equivalent in the gospel that could be applied to this domain. While Jesus might appear quite conservative in the institutional area, the gospels demonstrate a large openness in the domain of faith. The apostles are all male and of Jewish origin. With Paul and the Council of Jerusalem changes are made and, progressively, the gospel, and Luke in particular, demonstrate that salvation is brought to all nations and that no difference is to be made between men and women. Women are the first to witness the resurrection for instance. We cannot conclude from these remarks that Jesus was a social reformer. Nonetheless, if we understand access to salvation as essential to human dignity, then the universal access to salvation provides clear direction on how to refrain from discrimination.

While the above does not clearly and conclusively demonstrate a convergence between the Decent Work Agenda and the Christian tradition, we can detect some common background and commonalities, which can provide the basis for a dialogue between politicians and theologians. Lines of communication remain to be established and, before going much further, we need to clarify where and how this dialogue can happen in today's world.

## A place for dialogue

In many European countries, the USA and in some parts of Latin America, work has been part of the conversation between religions and politics. The Weberian situation, where religions and societies were in dialogue, created a space in which the conversation on labor could take place. Predominantly within Catholic countries, the social doctrine of the church, which is as much of a doctrine as it is a complex movement, has been one vehicle for this involvement. The other vehicle is most

---

[5] At **www.ilo.org/ilolex/cgi-lex/convde.pl?C111**.

probably the Christian labor movement, which, while never in a majority situation, nevertheless is sufficiently well organized to sit at the table. This conversation has been possible in the Netherlands, Belgium and Germany where Catholics have played a significant role. The parallel history of the role of the Protestant churches suggests a similar involvement in Switzerland and maybe also in the Nordic region.

Several forces of change are in the process of altering this landscape. The first one is secularization which has led to the secularization of the global Christian labor movement.

The second, and probably most important cause of change, are the forces of globalization and their underlying ideologies. Within the area of work, trade unions developed while the Christian trade unions were divided and lost momentum. At the same time, two ideologies that are sometimes unconscious allies developed in parallel: the Washington consensus and the development paradigm. Churches were very distant from and critical of the former, but embraced the development paradigm and the development cooperation movement. Churches created development agencies and organizations, in many instances loosely connected to the Christian labor movement. The Catholic Church distanced itself from this movement as is reflected in the papal encyclicals. During Pope Paul VI's papacy, the labor question became somewhat secondary, but Pope John Paul II, coming from a country with heavy industry and dealing with difficult social questions, put the question of labor back on the agenda of the Roman Catholic Church.

The third, but probably not last, force at play is the changing relationship between the local and the global, or rather the local, the regional and the global. This affects politics as well as religion. Within the world of religions, reactions vary from place to place. On the political and diplomatic scenes, new countries are emerging and certain political alliances are restricting access to circles of global power. In the religious world, the local and global expressions vary greatly. All kinds of systems prevail: from the aggregation of very local, almost parochial, organizations, to networks of experts, of leaders, as well as global associations. It is not always clear whether and where the Weberian model of distance and dialogue between religion and society is still at play

Last one should mention the dynamics created by interreligious forums at the local level. In places where conflicts, wars and violence have erupted, interreligious conferences and groups have played a significant role. In Africa and Asia, they have taken on a political role and have developed an interesting dynamic. As they have come to reflect on the root causes of conflicts, as well as on the power dynamics at play, they have also shown an interest in pursuing reflections on the world of labor. Their political legitimacy, often based on neutrality vis-à-vis corrupt power brokers and on the affirmation of common values where dialogue plays an important role, put them in a very interesting position. It would be possible for them to contribute to future dialogues on labor values.

## Questions to be addressed

In the following I shall list a number of questions that theologians might ask politicians, including trades unionists, employers' representatives, governments and parliamentarians and, vice versa, questions politicians might ask theologians. Some of them are directly linked to labor while others refer to the way in which the public sphere is currently organized.

### Questions to politics

"As a politician, do you consider that religions are a source of inspiration and motivation for people to contribute to societies and to the common good?" This question was raised by Pope Benedict XVI when he addressed the United Nations in 2008 and derives from an analysis and critique of the way in which public institutions allow for dialogue with religions. In some cases, the religious is relegated to the private sphere since there is the perception that the world would be better off without religion. This is linked to feelings of resentment or fear that everything in religious life is a first step to extremism or to a rejection of modernity. In others, religions are perceived as political forces or networks that need to be influenced or are worth instrumentalizing. In this case, religion is at the service of other ideologies. Stories about the complacency of religious institutions and dictatorships abound. Nonetheless, religions are also regarded as serving human rights or other humanitarian causes. The possibility of identifying convergences and common interests between religious groups and political entities is not to be denied, but the road toward establishing active, innovative, trusting and meaningful cooperation and dialogue between them still lies ahead of us. Much will depend on the goodwill and disposition of religious institutions on the one hand, and the political actors on the other.

"Do you believe in and act according to the principle that labor is not a commodity?" This principle has been strongly affirmed by the Catholic social doctrine as well as the Life and Work Movement[6] and is probably the best example of a religious contribution to the shaping of a cultural and political "imagination." Today political life is lacking in imagination, not merely ideas and motivation.

---

[6] Cf. http://en.wikipedia.org/wiki/World_Council_of_Churches.

Imagination in the sense that the complexities of life and situations that do not fit into the public discourse, are often simplified, and reduced to power games and relationships. The establishment of rights lacks the narratives of everyday life, where people can express their views, relate their experience and bring their testimony. Rights always risk becoming "abstractions" if there is no place in which to express the meaning of life when they are respected, and no place to express difficulties and atrocities and to talk about the inhumanity that they reveal. When the churches affirmed that labor is not a commodity, they referred to everything that was expected of work: the accomplishment of oneself and the service to others; the responsibility for one's own life; the commitment to one's family, nation, country and people. Labor is more than a commodity; it not only provides material sustenance, but nourishes a sense of dignity and responsibility and constitutes a commitment to creation. Moreover, factory workers, street vendors, farmers or bankers need a space where they talk about their life at work—their joy as well as their suffering; the meaning they find in their everyday work or the lack of such meaning when bad conditions prevail. Churches can provide the space where such narratives can be elaborated constructively.

## Questions to theology

"Are labor and economic life theological questions?" I have suggested above that labor can be part of the narratives developed among believers and within churches. This question goes one step further and suggests that it is possible to develop a theology of work. This has two implications: the first is ethical, the second theological. In the Christian traditions, there is room for ethics. The perception of work is ambiguous. Work is positive, connected to salvation and to the positive contribution of each individual to humanity, but can also negative, connected to or associated with alienation, difficulties, deprivation and slavery. The theological debate on work has a strong ethical dimension and we should discuss under what circumstances work is respectful of human dignity and contributes to the meaning of life. Potentially this could be of interest to politicians. Secondly, theological discourse could try to assess in which sense the experience of work is indeed part of the human experience of God and what it tells us of God. This dimension is probably only of secondary interest to politicians; however, in my view it is essential in order to guarantee a place for a theology of work within the global theological discourse.

"How does Christian theology reflect the Christian point of view?" In the public sphere, theologians are often critiqued and sometimes thought of as mere ideologues or extremists. They are believed to be ineffective—in political terms illegitimate—in the sense that their discourse is totally disconnected from people's lives. This critique invites us to reflect on how theological discourse is produced and how this discourse is connected to the life of the believer. If we understand theology as a form of interpretation, then this interpretation should encompass not only elements of the tradition and the community and the Scriptures, but also people's spiritual experience. This brings us back to the previous question. The legitimacy—in the political sense—of Christian theology depends on its ability to relate to the experience of the people. If we speak of a theology of labor, this would clearly mean that we incorporate in our theological reflection elements of our experience of work and what this experience tells us about God.

## Conclusion

In light of the present situation, the theology of labor is probably at a crossroads. On the one hand we have the heritage of theological reflection and perspectives from a world of labor, dominated by the industrial revolution and its aftermath, especially the "thirty glorious years," as well as the history of development and north—south relationships of which the churches have been a part. Moreover we must not forget the new context of globalization. On the other, developing a theology of work is not just about inheriting or adjusting to a new context. It is also about finding a practical path for theology at the crossroads of biblical studies, spirituality, practical theology and ethics. Dialogue is probably key: between theologians of various disciplines; theologians and believers; actors in different areas of the world economy; theologians and other actors from development agencies and other international institutions; unions and other places involved in the area of labor.

The challenge for believers and nonbelievers alike is to be able to develop a vision of labor, where human dignity is at the center and where economic exchange, power and greed are not perceived as the only rational human motivation and a vision of the world in which religions are a source of inspiration and motivation to act and contribute to greater social justice.

# Toward a Theology of Work from the Perspective of Women Migrants

## Roswitha Golder

Having spent nine-tenths of my life among people of cultures and languages different from my own, my own experience as a migrant and as a woman thus informs my reflections. For the past fourteen years, I have worked as a Protestant pastor ministering to migrant congregations in Geneva, Switzerland. My theology of work—and of migration—is rooted in this context. For most churches the concerns of migrants are not a priority, even if migrant churches constitute the fastest growing segment of Christianity. The church's official, public face is still largely, if not exclusively, male dominated, even though most of its members are women.[1] Their contributions through paid and unpaid labor are rarely acknowledged, yet without them neither church nor society would continue to function.

The Bible talks about work as a part of divine and human identity. God created the earth and human beings who are to take good care of it. Work is seen as an essential part of human nature and corresponds to God's original plan. Work confers dignity and gives meaning to human existence.[2]

Whereas the first creation narrative in Genesis does not take into account the problematic aspects of human activity, these are all the more present in the second. The acts of procreation on the part of the woman and of tilling the soil to obtain food on the part of the man are linked to strenuous efforts causing sweat and pain. Despite progress in medicine and agricultural technology, reproductive and productive work is not always pleasant, dignified, nor appreciated for its just value.

---

[1] The launch of the document "Christian Witness in a Multi-Religious World: Recommendations for Conduct" held at the Ecumenical Center on June 28, 2011 is an obvious example: the six speakers representing the World Council of Churches, the Pontifical Council for Interreligious Dialogue and the World Evangelical Alliance—which together account for ninety percent of the world's Christians—were men, mostly gray-haired, and all but one white Westerners.

[2] Claus Westermann, *Genesis Kapitel* 1–11 (Neukirchen-Vluyn: Neukirchener Verlag, 1983), 300ff. This part of my article is inspired by Nicolas Künzler's unpublished manuscript *"Mémoire de licence" L'être humain dans la creation, Étude de Gn 2–3, Gn 1 et Gn 6–9* (University of Geneva, September 1985).

After we moved to Geneva from Latin America almost thirty years ago, one of my husband's nephews—from the German-speaking part of Switzerland—came to live with us for the first year of his medical studies. When we laid down the rules of the household, I told him that I worked longer hours than my husband, even though his job also kept him busy beyond the usual nine to five schedule. Since the young man shook his head in disbelief, I proceeded to explain that, on top of my studies in theology, I took care of practically all the household chores. He admitted that he had never considered the latter— nor possibly the former— to be "work." Expressions such as "working mother"[3] tend to reinforce this dichotomy: remunerated work is rated as valuable to the economy, while other, non-paying jobs, although just as essential for human survival, do not normally figure in statistics and economic data.

Pastoral and other church work falls somewhere in between the categories of remunerated and volunteer work; it often belongs to both. In the industrialized societies, most pastors and lay employees receive salaries, even if on average these tend to be lower than those paid by the state and the private sector. Yet, the working hours required to do a good job often exceed those required of the professionals working for the state or in industry. Some churches expect their ministers, in addition to their paid service, to offer at least as many unpaid hours to the church as does the average lay volunteer.

The 2011 European Year of the Volunteer gives visibility to the often hidden, unpaid contributions women and men make to the economy. Efforts are being made to expand the scope of official statistics to include the countless hours people offer to their families, churches and to society through such service. Many migrant churches in particular depend on voluntary contributions in time and money, far beyond the commitment "normal" parishioners make to their congregations. These churches do not resemble the state churches in many parts of western Europe, nor do they conform to the prevalent ecclesial model in industrialized nations such as the USA, where the pastor's work is salaried, even though there is a clear division between church and state. Many pastors of the some seventy migrant congregations in Geneva hold full-time, secular jobs besides taking care of their flock. Only those employed by the handful of "historical" or "mainline" migrant churches are able to earn a living wage by ministering to their congregations. Others frequently have to rely on their spouse's income.

---

[3] This expression is commonly used for women who combine the responsibilities of motherhood with gainful employment outside the home in complete ignorance of the fact that "stay-at-home" or "unem-ployed" mothers also accomplish a considerable amount of—unpaid—work raising their children and taking care of their households.

Thus their situation resembles that of most of their parishioners: migrants, especially immigrants who lack official legal status, often work several shifts since they normally find themselves at the bottom of the salary scale. Women are doubly disadvantaged in this market. In Switzerland, women still earn about twenty percent less for comparable work than their male counterparts.[4] Yet, the so-called "sans papiers"[5] are mostly women, for whom there are more jobs available because Swiss employers prefer women to do household chores or to look after children or the elderly. Moreover, many men might refuse to accept some of the job conditions, i.e., the low wages, the long working hours, the lack of paid vacations, sleeping in the same room if not in the same bed as the employer's children, etc. The salaries of the "sans papiers" in the informal sector of the economy fail to appear in official government statistics, but many migrants send money back home. This makes up a large part of the hard currency flowing into such countries as Bolivia, China, Indonesia, or the Philippines.

All over the world, many "sans papiers" seek integration into a faith community upon their arrival. Some of them, especially those who speak the local language, manage to join "normal" local congregations that accept them as brothers and sisters in Christ. Sometimes they quickly join a voluntary church or community service organization. There where proof of successful integration is required this may be to their advantage when they seek to legalize their status. Some ask their pastor to write letters of recommendation confirming that they are active members or even leaders in their congregations; I always accompany such documents by prayer. This has sometimes had the desired effect.

Over the past thirty years numerous "new migrant churches" have sprung up all over Europe to meet the migrants' needs to worship in their own languages

---

[4] They are also relatively rare in top positions of private companies, and almost non-existent as professors of theology in this country.

[5] A term coined in France, but also widely used in Switzerland. It is applied to persons employed without the necessary permits to live and work in the country. It is not an appropriate description since normally "sans papiers" have all their personal documents such as passports, identity cards, etc. but they lack the appropriate legal status as workers. Some of them may have lost such permits when labor legislation changed and wanted to stay on in Switzerland. This applies to workers from the Balkans and Turkey, who were at one point legally employed as "seasonal workers." According to the bilateral agreements between Switzerland and the European Union, only citizens from EU countries are supposed to fill such positions. Some of the "sans papiers" are asylum seekers staying on after their request has been rejected. Others, especially from Africa, the Philippines and Latin America are "economic refugees," entering the country across the "green border" without registration, or as tourists staying on after permitted maximum of six months. In order to enter Switzerland successfully without being sent back upon arrival, or to be detained along the way for lack of proper documentation, the majority of the migrants pay for the services of so-called "passeurs," who assist them in avoiding border controls. Such "helpers" are often people from their own country residing legally in Switzerland. This kind of trafficking in human beings is a lucrative business until one gets caught. It leads to heavy sanctions: jail terms with subsequent expulsion from Swiss territory.

and in accordance with their own spiritualities. I have visited most of the seventy such churches in Geneva, most of which function under the leadership of a male pastor despite the majority of the congregation being female. There are some notable exceptions of very gifted women pastors doing an excellent job.

The fact that one finds fewer men in some of these migrant congregations does not necessarily reflect the same demographic reality found in the average Swiss church, where women far outnumber men during Sunday worship services. Because there are few job openings available for migrant men from Latin America and the Philippines, those migrant congregations have fewer men than some African, Sri Lankan and Chinese migrant congregations that show a more balanced attendance of men and women. Some may even have a majority of men, among them asylum seekers, refugees and "sans papiers."

In congregations made up mainly of expatriates working for international organizations or businesses the proportion of men sitting in the pews or taking responsibility for different congregational tasks tends to exceed the one in local churches. For example, in the Lutheran, Anglican and Episcopalian congregations in Geneva, the men seem to take just as active a part in church life as the women. Both "old" mainline (migrant) churches that have existed in Geneva for several centuries, as well as "new"—often charismatic or Pentecostal—migrant churches function as "free churches." They do not receive subsidies from the state but rely on voluntary contributions from their members in the form of cash,[6] goods and services. Both men and women are expected to contribute financially as well as through voluntary service to the church. Some migrant churches manage to finance missionary projects in their home countries or elsewhere in the world, including churches whose members include a large number of "sans papiers." Obliged to keep a low public profile in order to avoid the threat of being sent back to their home countries, many discover the church as a safe place where they not only receive spiritual nourishment, but are allowed and empowered to contribute visibly to the well-being of their community.[7] Migrant churches thus provide a spiritual home, offer their members the opportunity to make friends and provide valuable information regarding the new environment. These churches also encourage their members to use their talents and exercise leadership in volunteer and sometimes even paid work.

---

[6] Tithing, i.e., giving at least one tenth of one's income to the church, is expected and additional "sacrificial" contributions may be solicited. Some migrant churches collect several offerings during the same service; most place a special emphasis on generous giving. Prayers over the offering may include the request for employment, so that those members unable to contribute may do so in future.

[7] During the twelve years of my pastoral ministry to the Latin American community in Geneva, two of the women holding the office of president did not have a recognized legal status in Switzerland.

A booklet published jointly by "Camarada," a welcoming space for migrant women and their children, as well as "Voie F," an educational space for women, comprises testimonies of undocumented women who recently immigrated to Geneva. Under the title "My Open Doors," Dorkas writes,

> For me, open doors represent the opportunities I have had in my life. Before I left Bolivia, I prayed that all the doors I was dreaming about would open for me. The first one I passed is the one of my own country and that one is always open. The second one is my arrival in Geneva, via the airport, and I have lived here for the past several years. The third door I had to enter in order to survive was work. I found employment as a domestic worker. I had to clean a three-story house in one morning. This was too much for me, especially since I did not know how to use a vacuum cleaner. This door is closed now, but it has helped me open the fourth one. I realized that I had to learn French in order to get around in Geneva. A big thank you to Camarada for opening its doors to migrant women from all over the world.[8]

Much of what the Bible says about human experience is written from the perspective of individuals and groups on the move. "Migration is normal. The sedentary way of life constitutes an exception and a luxury, at least if we look at the larger geographical and chronological picture."[9] As mortals, human beings are but sojourners on the earth. God's people are a people on the move. Biblical stories take on new meaning when read with the eyes of migrants:[10]

The book of Ruth is a favorite among women who leave their countries because their families are starving, need financial help for an expensive operation, or support for the children's education. Famine, the cause of migration during Naomi's and Elimelech's time, continues to ravage many parts of the world. Ethnically and religiously mixed marriages, a consequence of migration then as well as now, continue to be a particular challenge to many couples. The only certain and relatively easy way for non-European citizens to legalize their status in Switzerland is through marriage to a Swiss citizen or to a person with a valid permit. This may lead to different types of abuse. Some of the situations, unfortunately, do not turn out as "positively" as Ruth's. I put

---

[8] Dorkas, "Mes portes ouvertes," in Camarada and Voie F, *Genève regards de migrantes* (2011), 39 (author's own translation).

[9] Benz H.R. Schär, "Höslis, Bünzlis und die Landverheissungen," in *vice-versa, Mitteilungen der Fachstellen Oekumene, Mission, Entwicklungszusammenarbeit* (OeMe) (2/2003), 16 (author's own translation).

[10] Cf. Daniel G. Groody and Gioacchino Campese (eds), *A Promised Land, A Perilous Journey. Theological Perspectives on Migration* (Notre Dame: University of Notre Dame, 2008).

positive in quotation marks, because it is the way most of us—possibly out of ignorance concerning the context—were taught to interpret the text. The story does not tell us how Ruth herself felt. Readers often overlook the fact that Naomi "took the child and laid him in her bosom, and became his nurse. The women of the neighborhood gave him a name, saying, 'A son has been born to Naomi'" (Ruth 4:16–17a). Thus Ruth completely disappears from the scene; the whole situation resembles that of migrant women used as surrogate mothers.[11]

Today, many women in Asia and Latin America pack their bags and go to find domestic employment notably in the Gulf States and in Europe. Many of them are "single mothers." Employment abroad means doing what they know how to do best, i.e., managing and running a household. Many of them raise their employer's offspring while their own—in the best case—are being cared for by neighbors and relatives, but sometimes left to fend for themselves on the street. Government agencies and non-governmental organizations are trying to stem the influx of "illegal" migrants expecting to overcome poverty by producing films depicting the reality in the "promised land:" the difficulty to find employment as well as the often dismal working conditions. When one of these films, produced in the Netherlands by an African immigrant, was shown at the recent general assembly of the Churches Commission for Migrants in Europe, in Bucharest, Rumania, participants were told that the situations portrayed would probably not have the desired effect of deterring people from leaving their home countries since their situations were so bad that they would do anything to escape. This, of course, is the case of people fleeing from civil war, political oppression or uprisings as well as those escaping a family feud or vendetta. But even migrants, not facing such situations, tell me that I have no idea what life for them was like and that I should refrain from judging whether or not they would have been better off staying at home.

Migrant workers thus tend to identify with the story of the patriarchs, starting with Abraham, whom God told to leave his country and promised a better future elsewhere. The fact that the latter was fraught with numerous delays, trials and tribulations, resonates with the experience of many migrants throughout history. It is interesting to note that the literal translation of God's command to Abraham in Genesis 12:1 reads, "Go for yourself" or "go towards yourself" as you leave the country of your birth and your father's house toward the land I will show you! Rabbinic exegesis has understood this to mean "go to find your own good, your happiness" and numerous are the migrants, especially women, who realize that only by leaving their homelands they were able

---

[11] I owe this insight to Dr Fulata Mbano Moyo, Women in Church and Society, World Council of Churches.

autonomously to shape their destiny. For many, leaving their home country provides an opportunity to go back to the roots of their faith. As they seek the company of fellow believers who worship in their own language and according to the well-known rituals, these religious traditions come alive and become more meaningful than they were back home, where they had been taken for granted. Prayer also takes on an urgent and practical side when things go awry and despair sets in. Weekly prayer meetings, regular all-night vigils, prayer chains, as well as prayer sought and offered by phone, are an integral part of the worship life of most migrant churches. Requests often refer to practical concerns such as health, housing, family problems or difficult job situations. Some also struggle with ethical issues such as sexual relations before marriage, couples living together without being married, or homosexuality, often a taboo in their home countries. Newer migrant churches, especially those from Africa, Asia and Latin America, tend to be more conservative in such matters than local churches or those with a predominantly European or North American constituency. This is one of the areas creating tensions and making ecumenical relationships difficult among migrant as well as local churches. Gender roles, distribution of labor in the home and the market place, the education of children and the freedom given to them, vary from one culture to another. In an effort to preserve their cultural heritage, first generation migrants frequently attempt to continue their way of life in the new context. Biblical texts taken literally serve as strict guidelines providing moral standards and infallible truths. Biblical stories such as Ruth and Esther provide a mirror to view one's own experience.

Through the ages, the necessity for people living in rural areas to find gainful employment outside agriculture has resulted in the migration from rural to urban contexts. In many parts of the developing world, rural areas do not receive the necessary attention by national politicians and often lack decent healthcare, schools and other community services. As a result, agriculture is not developed to its potential and the soil fails to nourish all its inhabitants.[12]

For centuries, people who grew up in the countryside have had to seek their fortune in the cities, sometimes even moving abroad. In medieval Europe, young men from the Alpine valleys were hired as mercenaries by opposing foreign powers with the result that family members fought against and killed one another. Adventurers still sign up for the French Foreign Legion. Dur-

---

[12] The "Commission protestante romande Suisse-Immigré-e-s" is working on a brochure detailing the effects of the global economic system that makes the (few) rich richer and the (many) poor poorer. The situation is particularly devastating for the small farmer, shop owner etc., not only in the global South but also in the industrialized nations.

ing the nineteenth and the first half of the twentieth centuries, impoverished Europeans moved to Africa, the Americas, Australia and New Zealand in search of a better life. Since the end of World War II, the tide has turned and migrants from other continents flock to Europe. Current public opinion, fuelled by the xenophobic propaganda of right-wing parties, sees this influx of foreigners as a threat to national security. This discourse fails to take into account that neither the formal nor the informal sector of the economy would function without the migrant labor force.

If first generation immigrants often intend to return to their home countries, second and third generations are more likely to settle in the new surroundings. In the process of growing roots away from home, the letter of Jeremiah to the exiles in Babylon, Jeremiah 29, inspires Christian immigrants.

> Build houses and live in them; plant gardens and eat what they produce. Take wives and have sons and daughters; take wives for your sons, and give your daughters in marriage, that they may bear sons and daughters; multiply there, and do not decrease. But seek the welfare of the city where I have sent you into exile, and pray to the Lord on its behalf, for in its welfare you will find your welfare... (Jer 29:5ff.).

Faithful to this teaching, practically all the migrant churches that I have visited regularly pray for Geneva. Many of them hold special revival meetings and evangelistic campaigns to reach the local population.[13] Members readily tell their employers about their faith and their commitment to their church. Some bring their charges to Sunday school and other appropriate activities organized by their congregations. Whereas employees of international companies and organizations manage to build homes, plant gardens and collect fruit from their trees in and around Geneva where they may even eventually retire, this luxury is not afforded those on the limited income of the average foreign worker, let alone of the "sans papiers," whose legal status precludes such plans for permanent residence abroad. However many of the former and even some of the latter manage to save enough money to purchase or to build a place to live back home, thus at least providing decent housing for their families. Whether and when they decide to move back "home" will depend on many factors, not least the work situation in their adopted country.

---

[13] "Reverse mission" or "Bringing back the gospel" are technical terms used to describe this phenomenon. See Claudia Währisch-Oblau, *The Missionary Self-Perception of Pentecostal/Charismatic Church Leaders from the Global South in Europe. Bringing Back the Gospel* (Leiden: Brill, 2009).

When the economic crisis hit Spain, many of the Latin American immigrants decided to return to their country of origin. Others profited from the fact that workers with European Union permits are allowed to seek employment in countries such as Switzerland. As a result the local job market is saturated. Moreover, following the downturn in the local job market, a number of households, which previously had two incomes, now have to manage with one. As a consequence, one of the partners who had previously held a job now stays at home and assumes the duties formerly done by the domestic help. Whether the situation will eventually change and people will continue hiring "sans papiers" and risk heavy fines remains to be seen.

In the meantime, men and women from countries newly admitted to the European Union, who can be legally employed, already fill some of these positions. They may possibly squeeze out domestic workers coming from other parts of the world. A lot remains to be done to protect the human rights of both the legal and "illegal" foreign workers in Switzerland and other industrialized nations. Racial and gender discrimination continues to be a problem and with the increasing gap between high and low incomes, migrant women with a low level of education still find themselves at the bottom of the salary scale. Both local and migrant churches are in a position to empower and accompany them as they assert their legal rights. Workers' unions at the local and national levels as well as the International Labour Organisation (ILO) have begun to take an interest in the domestic sector and are promoting minimum wages, regular working hours and holidays for men and women working in this largely informal, hidden sector of the economy.

Considerable patience and endurance will be required until these efforts bear fruit. Here the parable in Matthew 13:24–30 springs to mind.

The current political climate of many of the industrialized nations endangers the peaceful and just relations between men and women, migrants and established populations. Matthew's parable calls for the patient nurturing of just and inclusive relationships so that a climate of confidence and respect can grow until such a time when discord and rejection, sown by the enemy between men and women, young and old, people of different origins and social status, will no longer endanger the still fragile cooperation and mutual enrichment.

I regard the declaration of 2010 as the year of migration and 2011 as the year of the volunteer as hopeful signs, because these commemorations focus on aspects of the economy in general and labor in particular that are not normally in the public eye. They tend to receive only partial attention in secular publications and often remain outside the scope of theological research.[14] Yet a comprehensive theology of work in the twenty-first century is obliged to take into account both gender and migrant perspectives.

[14] Dietrich Werner made me aware of a notable exception. See Dietrich Werner, David Esterline, Namsoon Kang and Joshva Raja (eds), *Handbook of Theological Education in World Christianity* (Oxford: Regnum Books International, 2010). Pages 76–104 are dedicated to "Race, Power, and Migration in Theological Education." The first part, written by Henry S. Wilson and Werner Kahl, discusses "Global Migration and Challenges to Theological Education" (76–84), and the second, by Lester Edwin J. Ruiz, is dedicated to "Recovering the Body: When Race and Power Migrate." Both make for stimulating reading.

# The Theological Ethics of Work and Reward

## Edward Dommen

> Every problem related to wages is first of all a spiritual problem. God enjoins that wages should be shared among human beings by taking into account the bonds of community that unite them in accordance with God's will.[1]

In 2009, Credit Suisse's Chief Executive Officer Brady Dougan's annual income was CHF 90 million, 1812 times that of the bank's least paid employee. With CHF 43 million, 752 times that of the company's lowest paid employee, Daniel Vasella, chair of Novartis, was the second highest paid person in Switzerland.[2] The scandal of "rip-off" pay is thus not confined to the banks.[3]

It cannot be argued that Mr Dougan's own, unassisted efforts produce 1812 times more than those of any one of his colleagues. On the contrary, his output depends on the conjugated efforts of all his colleagues, the capital equipment with which they work, and the social capital, i.e., the way society at large is organized and run, which allow the bank to produce the services it provides. One would expect the owners of the capital, the shareholders, to be annoyed by this failure to recognize their contribution; indeed, thirty percent voiced their discontent at the bank's annual general meeting.

Social capital includes law and order—of particular relevance to banks—since Switzerland's twisted and selfish laws are especially designed to make it easy for Swiss banks to steal from other countries. I use "steal" in the way in which Calvin defines stealing, namely, that any means that we use to enrich ourselves at the expense of others should be regarded as theft.[4] It is common knowledge that Swiss banks thrive on attracting funds from clients anxious to avoid paying their due share of taxes in their own countries.

---

[1] André Biéler, *Calvin's Economic and Social Thought* (Geneva: World Alliance of Reformed Churches/ World Council of Churches, 2005), 369.

[2] At **www.24heures.ch/brady-dougan-gagne-1812-fois-salaries-2010-06-21**.

[3] A popular initiative against pay on this scale, "the Minder initiative," has collected the required number of signatures and is in the process of parliamentary treatment in Switzerland. Its Web site (**www.abzockerei.ch**), uses the term "rip-off" in the title of its English version.

[4] John Calvin, *Institutes of the Christian Religion*, at **www.reformed.org/master/index.html?mainframe=/ books/institutes/**, 2.8.45.

If Mr Dougan wishes to prove that his personal efforts are so lucrative, I suggest that he move his office to Mogadishu and see what happens to his output when it is really unassisted.

You do not have to take my word as a professional economist for the foregoing arguments. Even the executive committee of *Les Libéraux-Radicaux* (PLR) [the Swiss Liberal Radical Party], a conservative party, sympathetic to business interests, said that Brady Dougan's salary bore no relation to the work furnished.[5]

It is sometimes taken for granted that such an immense salary is not a reward as such for the CEO's productive efforts but rather reflects their presumed influence on the company's share price. It is assumed that the share price is what primarily, if not exclusively, concerns the shareholders. Therefore, if one accepts that the company is at the service of its shareholders, the CEO deserves to be rewarded according to their influence on the share price.

This assumption, namely that the company is beholden only to its shareholders, has been contested by those who maintain that the company has an obligation to all its stakeholders.[6] The list of stakeholders is open ended, including the employees, suppliers, consumers, different levels of government, as well as people affected by the externalities of the company's activities, not to mention the environment.

On the other hand, even if we accept the ideology according to which the senior management is to serve the interests of shareholders exclusively, we still need to establish the extent to which the share price can be attributed to the CEO's individual effort. Indeed, share prices fluctuate as a result of a wide range of factors, amongst which one can single out the following:

- Data concerning the company's activities, whether published by the company itself or other sources
- Official statements by the company
- Unofficial statements which have their source within the company
- Rumors
- Irrelevant but iconic statistics such as the quarterly unemployment figures released by the US government have a widespread effect on share prices in other countries.

---

[5] ATS, quoted by Radio Suisse Romande, **www.rsr.ch/#/info/les-titres/economie/1891120**.

[6] See the Wikipedia article "Stakeholder (corporate)." The Swiss ethically sustainable shareholder movement Actares (**www.actares.ch**), grandchild of the shareholder association Canes founded by André Biéler among others, firmly espouses this position.

The public is assured that it is the market that establishes the price of all traded goods and services, including those of the CEO. Nevertheless, whatever we are told, the market is not an impersonal precision instrument. Brady Dougan's salary is actually determined by a compensation committee composed of four persons: the chair of Swiss Re; the chair of Nestlé (the highest paid chair of any food company in the world); president and CEO (the same person) of the Olayan Group, a private multinational enterprise engaged in distribution, manufacturing and global investment; and the president and CEO of AIG (again a single person). AIG, notorious for its role in the recent US financial crisis, was generously bailed out by the US taxpayer.

We must note that half of the people who determine Dougan's salary are simultaneously CEOs and chairs of the board of a corporation. In other words, as chairperson they are responsible for supervising their own work as CEO. The acceptance of unsupervised behavior of this kind is at odds with what are becoming internationally recognized norms of good corporate governance.

All in all, one may have some serious doubts about the moral authority of those who decide Dougan's remuneration. Calvin said the following about fair remuneration, "Let us not consider what is allowable in terms of received common custom, nor assess what is right and fair by the iniquitous standards of the world"[7]—and even less so, surely, by those of one's cronies.

If it is legitimate for the CEO's salary to be determined by a small group of cronies, surely it is equally legitimate for the workers' wages to be determined independently by the workers themselves without previous consultation, let alone negotiation, with any other stakeholders. That would be no more than an application of the Golden Rule, "In everything do to others as you would have them do to you; for this is the law and the prophets." This fundamental rule of conduct can be found in countless religious and ethical traditions.[8] In Matthew 7:12, Jesus stresses that it "is the law and the prophets."

Brady Dougan's salary is no more than an expression of pride. The year 1812 marked the furthest reach of Napoleon's arrogance. It was then that the emperor's conquering armies were turned back from Moscow. Let us hope that Dougan's 1812 will mark the furthest reach of the arrogance of the "fat cats" who draw huge pay checks. Such remuneration is no more than a rude gesture of pride.

In the Catholic tradition, pride counts as one of the seven deadly sins. It is often considered as the original and most serious of the seven deadly sins and

---

[7] John Calvin, "Letter to Claude de Sachin (1545)," in M. Beaty, and B. W. Farley (eds), *Calvin's Ecclesiastical Advice* (Edinburgh: T. & T. Clark, 1991), 139–143.

[8] See, for instance, **www.unification.net/ws/theme015.htm**, consulted on 27.03.2011

the source of the other six. It is identified as the desire to be more important or attractive than others: the failure to acknowledge the good work of others and excessive love of self (especially in relation to God). Dante's definition was "love of self perverted to hatred and contempt for one's neighbour."[9] Calvin deals with all the foregoing in his usual terse, blunt style: "God ... abominates all luxury, pride, ostentation and vanity."[10]

The disproportionate income of some few, rare individuals panders to most if not all of the characteristics of pride in the recipient and the way in which company chiefs get together to fix each other's pay is an expression of their pride.

The Bible and Reformed theology lead us to think of reward in a way that is diametrically opposed to the current view and practices related to wages. Echoing Clavin, Biéler states that, "For them reward is part of the fruits of common work and of the property God grants to human beings ... for their maintenance."[11]

> Each individual should consider what he has, for in line with your resources you are obliged to recompense those who have worked for you and have been the means of such a blessing... If [God] has sent us servants to increase our resources, we are only shamming when we give thanks with our lips but despise those God has sent to work for us.[12]

Indeed, to accept for oneself a share that is out of all proportion to that of one's fellow workers is to mock them.

The PLR correctly points out that excessive bonuses undermine popular support for our liberal economic system. These huge rewards scandalize people and to benefit from inequality on this scale is provocative. Like the psalmist in Psalm 23:5, "You prepare a table before me in the presence of my enemies; you anoint my head with oil; my cup overflows."

After the issue of pride, scandal is the second theological point in this argument. Paul insists on not scandalizing but, on the contrary, edifying, i.e., striving to build a community which holds together:

> Let us therefore no longer pass judgment on one another ... nothing is unclean in itself; but it is unclean for anyone who thinks it unclean. If your brother or sister is being injured by what you eat, you are no longer walking in love. Do

---

[9] **http://en.wikipedia.org/wiki/Seven_deadly_sins**

[10] Calvin, op. cit. (note 4), 3.10.5

[11] Biéler, op. cit. (note 1), 368

[12] Calvin's sermon on Deuteronomy 15.

not let what you eat cause the ruin of one for whom Christ died. So do not let
your good be spoken of as evil. For the kingdom of God is not food and drink
but righteousness and peace and joy in the Holy Spirit. ... Let us then pursue
what makes for peace and for mutual upbuilding. ... We who are strong ought
to put up with the failings of the weak, and not to please ourselves. Each of
us must please our neighbor for the good purpose of building up the neighbor
[i.e., the edification of the community] (Rom 14:13–17, 19; 15:1–2).

In the end, it is perhaps not St Paul who speaks best to the condition of the
fat cats, but the Marquis de Sade: "It is very sweet to scandalize: it is a little
triumph for pride which is not to be scorned."[13]

In 2010, Brady Dougan was no longer the highest paid member of Credit
Suisse's executive board. He was surpassed by Antonio Quintella, CEO of
the Americas region, who earned CHF 15.63 million compared to Dougan's
mere CHF 12.76.[14]

The trade union organization Travail Suisse regularly publishes a league
table of the most unequal salary ranges in Swiss companies. In 2010, the two
big banks still beat all others: the ratio between the average income of members of the executive board and the worst paid employee was 1:207 at Credit
Suisse and 1:137 at UBS. The pharmaceutical company Roche came third at
1:114.[15] It should be noted that in 2010 Credit Suisse, like UBS, published
the amounts received by each member of the board of directors and the total
amount received by the executive board, but gave figures only for some of the
individual members. While no figures were published for other employees, it
is widely reported that certain employees, some traders for instance, receive
such large amounts that they also count among the fat cats.

The arguments against pride and scandal presented above apply to all these
cases. Perhaps scandal more than pride, though. Although it sounds paradoxical,
both of the big Swiss banks mention collaboration and teamwork among the
factors taken into account in fixing individual bonuses. In 2011, *The Economist*
reported on Boris Groysberg's fascinating study of successful Wall Street analysts who move from one firm to another, which revealed that when analysts
switch companies they see an immediate decline in their performance. For all

---

[13] "Il est très doux de scandaliser : il existe là un petit triomphe pour l'orgueil qui n'est nullement à
dédaigner," in Marquis de Sade, *La Philosophie dans le boudoir* (1795), at **http://fr.wikisource.org/wiki/
La_Philosophie_dans_le_boudoir**.

[14] *Credit Suisse Annual Report 2010*, 196. According to the same source, Mr Dougan received CHF 19.2
million in 2009.

[15] **www.travailsuisse.ch/fr/system/files/Annexes+CP+manager.pdf**.

their swagger, it seems that their success depends as much on their coworkers as on their innate talents. [16]

High salaries serve shareholders and the employees themselves rather than the customers or the public. Credit Suisse presents its compensation policy framework in two sentences:

> Our vision: Maintain a responsible, performance-based compensation policy that is aligned with the long-term interests of our employees and shareholders.
>
> Our promise: Strike the right balance between meeting shareholders' expectations, paying our employees competitively and responding appropriately to the regulatory environment.[17]

UBS states that, "Profitability is the main basis of our compensation funding,"[18] The general spirit of the report is similar to that of Credit Suisse although less explicit. As for the public interest, UBS talks about "exhibit[ing] professional and ethical behavior," "a high level of integrity," and, more ominously, "compliance with UBS policies."[19] Credit Suisse talks more vaguely, but no less ominously, about "recogniz[ing] the group's company values."[20]

Basically, the banks argue that they must pay their employees what it takes to attract and to keep them. Both name other large international banks which they use as benchmarks when fixing their employees' salaries. Whether or not the banks' customers benefit from the services rendered is not one of the considerations mentioned. Indeed, there appears to be no relationship between the banks' profitability and their ability to invest their customers' funds to the latter's profit. In an amusing article, *The Economist* reported on a study which concluded that poker is a game of skill: of the 32 000 players who took part in the 2010 World Series of Poker in Las Vegas, while "ordinary players made a loss of 15.6 percent, the skilled made a return on investment of 30.5 percent."[21] The authors say that similar tests have been used on mutual fund managers (a profession similar to that of the bankers in question in this paper). There seems to be "little evidence of skill in their domain."[22] A scathing article in the *Tribune de Genève* argues that the collective management of

---

[16] *The Economist*, 21 May 2011, 72.

[17] Ibid., 185.

[18] UBS, *Our Compensation in 2010*, 21

[19] Ibid., 9.

[20] https://www.credit-suisse.com/governance/en/compensation.jsp.

[21] *The Economist*, 19 May 2011, at www.economist.com/node/18713538.

[22] Ibid.

wealth destroys some USD 1 300 billion every year through fees, brokerage charges, commissions and other costs, in return for a performance well under that of the market average.[23]

One wonders why the customers tolerate this situation. After all, it is not unusual for investment funds to charge management fees of 1½—2 percent, which takes a significant chunk out of the amounts savers entrust to them.

One of the greatest achievements of the years following World War II in the global North was the establishment of a system of social security which assured a revenue to those whose capacity to earn was compromised by illness, disability, unemployment or, last, but certainly not least, old age.

The Bible refers to two ways of dealing with individual misfortune. One is to build up private reserves:

> Then he told them a parable: "The land of a rich man produced abundantly. And he thought to himself, 'What should I do, for I have no place to store my crops?' Then he said, 'I will do this: I will pull down my barns and build larger ones, and there I will store all my grain and my goods. And I will say to my soul, Soul, you have ample goods laid up for many years; relax, eat, drink, be merry.' But God said to him, 'You fool! This very night your life is being demanded of you. And the things you have prepared, whose will they be?' So it is with those who store up treasures for themselves but are not rich toward God" (Lk 12:16–21).

The parable dramatically exposes the inefficiency of the rich person's method. Admittedly, its argument rests on the unpredictability of individual life expectancy. Today's private pension schemes solve that by pooling the entitlements of the different participants on the basis of an average life expectancy estimated statistically: those who die sooner subsidize those who live longer. Thus, even the pension schemes founded on private accumulation are actually rooted in a form of social solidarity.

Deuteronomy 15 firmly urges:

> If there is among you anyone in need, a member of your community in any of your towns within the land that the Lord your God is giving you, do not be hard-hearted or tight-fisted toward your needy neighbor. You should rather open your hand, willingly lending enough to meet the need, whatever it may be (Deut 15:7–8).

---

[23] Marian Stepczynski, in *Tribune de Genève*, 16 May 2011, 4.

And it hammers the point home, "Since there will never cease to be some in need on the earth, I therefore command you, 'Open your hand to the poor and needy neighbor in your land'" (Deut 15:11).

And Matthew explains:

> Lord, when was it that we saw you hungry and gave you food, or thirsty and gave you something to drink? And when was it that we saw you a stranger and welcomed you, or naked and gave you clothing? ... And the king will answer them, "Truly I tell you, just as you did it to one of the least of these who are members of my family, you did it to me" (Mt 25: 37–40).

In the early years of social security, old age pensions were basically paid by redistribution: today's workers paid pension contributions which were more or less directly transferred to today's pensioners. With the rise of neoliberalism, the fashion changed. Old age comes inexorably to all those fortunate enough to reach it. It can be seen coming well in advance and its incidence can be estimated statistically with a high degree of probability. People were encouraged, indeed obliged, to build up a capital sum that was intended to generate the income which would, when the time came, pay their individual pensions. Large sums thus accumulated looked for a profitable place to go while waiting to be spent. As a result, the professions of wealth management expanded in order to handle this influx of capital. Individualism was the ideology underlying this shift. It was argued that if your pension depended on your own private savings, then you were free from entanglements with anyone else. This is a specious argument: apart from the actuarial consideration we have already mentioned, the income accruing from one's securities depends on how all the other parties involved in generating the total income, as well as oneself, decide on how to share it out at the time when it is actually shared out. The same argument applies not only to the income from one's securities, but also to their price should one wish to sell them. One knows how much one has put into one's savings, but how much they are worth at a later point depends on what others are at that point willing to pay for them.

The main result of sending pension contributions via investment in financial instruments on their way to becoming pensions is to enable the fat cats of finance to collect a substantial toll on the way. As John Donne said, no one is an island. There is no getting away from the fact that "we, who are many, are one body in Christ, and individually we are members one of another" (Rom 12: 5). Even the neoliberal Margaret Thatcher, immediately after her memorable declaration that "there is no such thing as society," went on to say that "It is our duty to look after ourselves and then also to help look after our neighbor and life is a reciprocal business."[24]

Let me conclude by saying that community is the leitmotiv underlying all the foregoing. It is the most fundamental theological point of this argument. Pride perverts the values of community by exploiting them: it needs an audience. As Psalm 23:5 stresses: "You prepare a table before me in the presence of my enemies;" scandal undermines community: "If your brother or sister is being injured by what you eat, you are no longer walking in love" (Rom 14:15). "Each of us must please our neighbor for the good purpose of building up the neighbor" (Rom 15:2). The refusal to recognize that we are members of one another is that which has enabled the proud and scandalous to indulge their fancy.

Let us not forget that the way in which salaries are determined is also a spiritual issue and touches on some of the most central issues of moral theology, not only in Christianity. Theology has its own contribution to make to this issue.

---

[24] Interview with *Woman's Own*, 31 October 1987, **www.margaretthatcher.org/document/106689**.

# The Impact of the HIV and Aids Epidemic on the World of Work and Development

Veikko Munyika

## Introduction

The HIV and AIDS epidemic affects all dimensions of human life; no individual or family, no organization or institution is spared. Because of its magnitude, the HIV and AIDS epidemic has become a top priority, within the economic as well as the development spheres. How does it impact the world of labor? Does it affect growth and, if so, how? In this paper I shall argue that the HIV and AIDS epidemic challenges the world of labor, slows down growth and reverses developmental gains. The major sources of this slowdown in growth are identified as (1) reduced productivity; (2) reduced population growth and human capital accumulation; and (3) reduced physical capital accumulation. Finally, I shall put forward some suggestions as to how to respond to the HIV and AIDS epidemic in regard to labor force, growth and development.

## The HIV and AIDS epidemic ravages the labor force

The HIV and AIDS epidemic has developed into a formidable challenge affecting the entire world, especially the developing nations where the prevalence of HIV and AIDS is the highest. It is no longer only a health issue but a substantial threat to socioeconomic development, imposing a heavy burden on families, communities and eventually on national economies. The impact of the pandemic is already evident in most countries of the world. In November 2010, UNAIDS announced that by 2009 more than 33 million persons were HIV positive worldwide. Most of them were workers aged between fifteen and forty-nine. This means that the most productive age group is also the most affected. This has consequences, not only for individuals, but for families, communities and national economies in terms of income, employment and changes on the labor market.

The economically active population constitutes the labor force, and without considering the particular impact that HIV and AIDS have on them, interventions designed to support employment, economic policy and national HIV and AIDS strategy cannot be implemented successfully. In the long run, the cost of inaction will be too high. To date, not enough is known about the impact of the epidemic on the structure and composition of the labor force.

A number of studies evaluating the impact of the HIV and AIDS epidemic on African economies have been carried out, focusing in particular on the macroeconomic aspects. Anne I. Odetola has surveyed influential literature on the subject. She writes,

> Theoretical and Empirical Review have attempted to evaluate the impact of the pandemic on African economies focusing on its macroeconomic aspects. Examples that have dominated the literature of studies in this aspect are by Kambou et al. (1992) using a CGE approach for Cameroon. Arndt and Lewis (2000) used the same approach for South Africa and Cuddington (1993) did the same analysis using data from Tanzania. However, the theoretical backing of the impacts of HIV/AIDS is best illustrated by Cohen (1993), who showed that HIV/AIDS affects the economy quantitatively and qualitatively.
>
> Furthermore, Ainsworth and Over (1994) stated that AIDS affects the structure, composition of the active labour force and increases morbidity and mortality thus destroying the basis for growth of potential output and productivity.[1]

These studies provide evidence for the International Labour Office's (ILO) conclusion that "AIDS ravages labour forces."[2]

According to the 2004 ILO survey, globally an estimated 36.5 million people engaged in some form of economic activity were HIV positive. Seventy percent of the world's HIV positive labor force was and still is in Africa. Their situation resulted in an annual loss of USD 25 billion in productivity. At the time, the ILO immediately warned that this was "just a start" because it was expected that "the number of infected workers and the consequent loss of productivity will climb sharply" to "reach 28 million" by 2005. "The figure could climb to 48 million by 2010 and 74 million by 2015.[3]

---

[1] Anne I. Odetola, *HIV/AIDS and the Nigerian Labour Force: A Descriptive Analysis* (2007), at **http://unpan1.un.org/intradoc/groups/public/documents/idep/unpan026137.pdf**.

[2] South African Institute of International Affairs, "AIDS Ravages Labour Force," in *eAfrica*, vol. 2 (August 2004), at **www.saiia.org.za/archive-eafrica/aids-ravages-labour-force.html**.

[3] DCOMM, Communication and Public Information, "First global analysis: HIV/AIDS to have major impact on world of work," in *World of Work Magazine*, no. 52, at **www.ilo.org/global/publications/magazines-and-journals/world-of-work-magazine/articles/WCMS_081336/lang--en/index.htm**.

Responding to the question of whether the HIV and AIDS pandemic increases or decreases growth in Africa, René Bonnel concluded that it clearly decreases growth, especially in countries having to deal with the additional challenge of malaria. Unfortunately, such reduction is larger when compared with the historical growth. Poverty, inequality, gender inequality, labor mobility and ethnic fractionalization are some of the factors driving the HIV and AIDS epidemic. However, Bonnel has it that "what has enabled HIV/AIDS to undermine economic and social development is the erosion of the main determinants of economic growth such as social capital, domestic savings and human capital."[4] Because HIV and AIDS prevent maximum participation of the labor force in economic development, it goes without saying that the HIV and AIDS epidemic increases poverty; poverty, in turn, accelerates the spread of HIV.

HIV and AIDS have become two of the worst killers among all known infectious diseases. Consequently, the world is experiencing a major development crisis. In Africa, for instance, HIV and AIDS related diseases are the main cause of mortality. The average life expectancy has been considerably reduced (i.e., southern Africa) in nearly all the countries where HIV and AIDS continue to spread.

## The HIV and AIDS epidemic undermines physical, human and social capital

The HIV and AIDS epidemic's extraordinary impact on development is a result of the epidemic's ability to undermine three main determinants of economic growth, namely, physical, human and social capital. These factors explain why HIV and AIDS have a major, direct effect on economic growth and social development.

> *HIV/AIDS reduces the stock of human and physical capital*, because it affects primarily the adult population in its most productive years, and it undermines its incentives to save and invest. The result is that the first-round reduction in human capital caused by AIDS-related deaths is further amplified over time by reduced incentives to invest in human capital.
>
> *AIDS destroys social capital because it is tearing away at existing institutions*. At the local level, AIDS is destroying the social fabric of communities. At the national level, AIDS is undermining the capacity of governments to provide basic social

---

[4] René Bonnel, "HIV/AIDS: Does it increase or Decrease Growth in Africa?," in World Bank, *AC-TAfrica* (2000), at **http://siteresources.worldbank.org/INTAFRREGTOPHIVAIDS/Resources/ Growth_in_Africa.pdf.**

services and efficient economic management, regulation and legal framework. The main economic effect is to reduce the efficiency of production and to lower output. This effect is probably recent, but it is likely to become more important over time.

*Feedback effects further amplify the impact of HIV/AIDS on economic growth.* If left unchecked, the HIV epidemic undermines some of the main determinants of growth, which in turn facilitates the spread of the HIV epidemic and further magnifies the initial impact of HIV on economic growth.

As a consequence of the long incubation period of the HIV virus (7-10 years), the impact of the HIV/AIDS epidemic is drawn over time with the rate of growth of physical and human capital falling down gradually, and the efficiency of social capital declining slowly. Over time, the behavior of GDP would reflect a similar gradual downward adjustment showing up as a reduction in the rate of growth of GDP rather than a sudden fall in GDP per capita.[5]

With regard to how HIV and AIDS affect economic growth, Bonnel has put forward the following two hypotheses:

HIV/AIDS reduces the growth rate of per capita income because: (i) it leads to a fall in the growth rate of labor and capital; and (ii) it generates a downward shift in the overall production function due to the erosion of institutions and policies that are crucial for economic growth.

The second hypothesis is that the impact of the HIV epidemic on growth has been amplified by the feedback effects that occur as part of the process of development.[6]

## Some channels through which HIV and AIDS affect economic growth

According to Bonnel's hypotheses, HIV and AIDS lead to economic and social stagnation.

*Macroeconomic policy.* Sound fiscal, monetary and exchange rate policies have consistently been found to be extremely important for growth. The hypothesis is that HIV/AIDS adversely affects macroeconomic outcomes because it worsens fiscal deficits and reduces the macroeconomic management capacity of governments.

---

[5] Ibid., 3.

[6] Ibid., 4.

*Physical capital*. Initially, the HIV/AIDS epidemic has a negligible impact on physical investment. Over time investment would be affected to the extent the HIV epidemic worsens the government budget and reduces domestic savings. The fiscal deficit is likely to worsen because of increased expenditures. [7]

Whether at the level of individuals, families, governments or institutions (insurance companies for instance), expenditures will increase due to the treatment and care of AIDS-related needs and challenges. Faced with the illness of adult family members, households experience a drop in income, which forces them to deplete their savings and/or assets. So far, this seems to have been the predominant development.[8]

HIV and AIDS are likely aversely to affect poor households in particular, which are often forced to resort to harmful survival strategies, including discontinuing the education of children, particularly girls. This increases the likelihood that the children will later earn lower incomes if they find employment at all. Their contribution to economic growth will only be minimal. This is confirmed by the ILO which states that,

> Children will suffer from a lack of parental care and guidance, or find themselves forced to abandon schooling and seek work which not only threatens their physical well-being but will deprive them of education, skills and training, thus threatening the goals of eliminating child labour and promoting sustainable development.[9]

For governments and other financial institutions, increased expenditures result from the many pension pay-outs for AIDS related deaths among civil servants and other customers as well as from the training costs of newly hired staff. This includes the training of teachers and health professionals who replace those who are either taking early retirement or have died prematurely. It is important for companies and organizations to keep in mind that dead people do not work and sick employees cost the employer money. It is less costly to invest in prevention and treatment. As the study of the ILO concludes,

> HIV/AIDS destroys human capital built up over years and weakens the capacity of workers to produce goods and services for the economy. This loss of skilled labour, together with the increase in care and treatment costs, tends to depress production, hamper savings and impede investment in the long run.[10]

---

[7] Ibid., 4.

[8] Cf. Ibid., 4.

[9] Op. cit. (note 3), 4.

[10] Op. cit. (note 2).

The HIV and AIDS epidemic destroys human capital more quickly than physical capital. This is particularly evident there where adequate information on HIV and AIDS is absent or where the impact of stigma, shame, denial, discrimination, inaction and "misaction" (SSDDIM) is ignored or underplayed. In such situations "both high and low-income groups were infected" and "a generation of educated civil servants, teachers, health workers and professionals is being lost."[11]

One of the determinants of growth is social capital. Trust and civil cooperation matter for economic growth. By affecting the social structure of local communities, HIV erodes existing social networks and traditional support mechanisms. Because HIV and AIDS reduce the skilled labor force, they negatively affect the ability of institutions, especially governments, to enforce effective regulations and legal frameworks.

## The main economic and social determinants of HIV and AIDS

We have referred to the channels through which HIV and AIDS can undermine the determinants of growth. We must now, unfortunately, also say that the same factors that can challenge economic development are key to the further spread of the HIV epidemic. Explaining the interconnection between HIV and growth, Bonnel states that,

> The result can be a vicious development cycle whereby HIV/AIDS undermines the main determinants of growth, which in turn facilitates the spread of the HIV epidemic and further reduces economic growth.[12]

The higher the prevalence of HIV and AIDS in a country, the slower its economic growth. There where the prevalence among the adult population is high, as for instance in southern Africa (Botswana 24.8, Lesotho 23.6, Malawi 11.0, Mozambique 11.5, Namibia 13.1, South Africa 17.8, Swaziland 25.9, Zambia 13.5, Zimbabwe 14.3,) economic growth would be the slowest.

> The economic impact of HIV/AIDS will not be uniform across countries or even within countries. Countries that are well developed with a strong health infrastructure can usually mobilize the resources needed to prevent early on the rapid spread of HIV/AIDS. They can take advantage of a widespread

---

[11] Op. cit. (note 4), 5.

[12] Ibid., 8.

medical infrastructure to dispense the medication that can allow HIV-infected individuals to remain engaged in economic activities. Furthermore, because of their well-developed educational system and stock of human capital, the AIDS-related loss of human capital does not entail the same consequences it has in countries where skilled labor is already in short supply.

By contrast, countries which do not have such resources are particularly vulnerable to a rapid spread of HIV and a subsequent vicious downward circle. This is especially true for countries with already weak social capital, which gets further eroded by the spread of HIV/AIDS.[13]

This same scenario can be applied at the household level. The poorer the family the more vulnerable to HIV it is and the severer the impact on it.

In such an environment, a vicious cycle is set in motion whereby lower growth increases poverty. With the infection of adults in families, breadwinners fall ill and stop earning. Children are then often taken out of school to look after the sick members of the families, which sharply constrains children's opportunities for higher income later in life. In such circumstances, the poor are forced to reduce their expenditure on food, which reduces further their resistance to the opportunistic infections resulting from HIV/AIDS. The consequences are increased poverty and the reversal of most development gains.[14]

## Increasing the economic immunity to HIV and AIDS

The interrelationships between the HIV and AIDS pandemic and economic development are extremely complex.

While HIV/AIDS reduces economic growth, economic growth can increase or decrease the spread of the HIV epidemic. On one hand, economic development can slow down the spread of the HIV epidemic. This is most likely when economic growth leads to rapid increase in education, especially female education, general improvement in physical infrastructure (which improves access to health and safe water), and employment opportunities for women. On the other hand, the process of economic development can facilitate the spread of the HIV epidemic. This is particularly the case if development is associated

---

[13] Ibid., 17.

[14] Ibid., 17.

with substantial labor migration within and among countries, investment in large projects, and political changes that result in social changes.[15]

What separates this two alternative outcome is how long the HIV epidemic has been on-going without any nation-wide HIV prevention activities. A key implication of infectious diseases is that they tend to spread exponentially in the population once some threshold is reached. The implication is that the growth effects of the HIV epidemic will be more pronounced the older the HIV epidemic. These effects include: (i) lower school enrollment; (ii) higher income inequality (because it rises with lower economic growth); (iii) fewer employment opportunities for women in the modern sector; and (iv) less investment in physical (and medical) infrastructure. The lack of early HIV prevention activities therefore increases the likelihood of a vicious cycle of underdevelopment.[16]

Like "misaction," inaction early on makes it difficult to provide the necessary services such as care, support, treatment and education later on when these are crucial for saving lives. Further, once the prevalence of HIV reaches a high level, the expenditure on necessary interventions, treatment, care and support of AIDS patients increase dramatically. While high-income countries can afford to meet such sky rocketing budgetary costs, most of the low-income countries will not manage on their own without external financial support. Only those countries that have early on invested enough in prevention strategies and have kept new infections at bay will be an exception. This means, keeping the number of new infections at a low level ensures that the future number of AIDS patients will be low and the cost of caring and treating them may be affordable.

## How should we respond?

There are numerous possible strategies to respond to HIV and AIDS in the world of work. The ILO established a special program in 2001, and drafted *An ILO code of practice on HIV/AIDS and the world of work* to provide a set of guidelines to address the HIV/AIDS epidemic in the world of work. [17] In line with these, the following may form part of the proposed plan of action in regard to mitigating the impact of HIV and AIDS in the world of work:

---

[15] Ibid., 18.

[16] Ibid., 18.

[17] At **www.ilo.org/wcmsp5/groups/public/@ed_protect/@protrav/@ilo_aids/documents/ normativeinstrument/kd00015.pdf.**

- The workplace as a point of entry: the workplace provides a vital entry point for the provision of education, care and treatment and activities to combat discrimination. Governmental, non-governmental (NGOs) and faith based organizations (FBOs) should endeavor to mainstream HIV and AIDS in the world of work and to give the epidemic the highest priority. In this way, the workplace takes centre stage in fighting the HIV and AIDS epidemic.

- Legislation and workplace policies: It helps for governments to draft enlightened legislation in the form of revised or new laws which can play an important role in mitigating the impact of HIV/AIDS at the workplace and protecting the rights of persons who are living with HIV/AIDS. Non-governmental and faith based organizations should develop workplace policies to guide processes by which strategies to respond to the HIV and AIDS epidemic are designed and implemented. Workplace policies also guide efforts to reduce stigma and discrimination, promote behavioral change, improve communication for personnel and ensure implementation of education and treatment programs. Legislation and workplace policy are regarded the least costly option to maintain profitability and to ensure growth.

- Maximum and meaningful involvement of PLWHIA [People living with HIV and AIDS]: For a meaningful and effective response to the HIV and AIDS epidemic, it is important to harvest the first-hand experience of people living with HIV. They are our "wounded healers" and sources of vital information. It pays to increase their maximum and meaningful involvement in the planning and implementation of workplace program.

- Affirmation of the *ILO Code of practice on HIV/AIDS and the world of work*: It is necessary for governments, NGOs and FBOs to reaffirm that *ILO code of practice on HIV/AIDS and the world of work* provides a framework for workplace action, and the promotion of good practice in policy formulation and program implementation.

- Empowerment of women: The impact of the HIV and AIDS epidemic is especially severe on women, who are more vulnerable than men and traditionally bear a heavier burden in caring for sick family members. This in turn decreases the amount of time women spend either in formal employment or in traditional roles such as subsistence agriculture. Their vulnerability to and infection by HIV directly or indirectly negatively impact economic growth and national development. Young women are now showing the largest increases in HIV infection.

Finally, across most of Africa, women are responsible for subsistence farming. If they themselves are not ill, the burden of caring for sick family members, the pressure to earn an income to replace the lost income of the person living with AIDS, and the burden of care for other family members—notably young children and older persons—may take away time for farming, which jeopardizes their capacity to provide food for the household, and/or ensuring the well-being of all household members. Thus, the empowerment of women is a preventive measure, both in terms of the further and rapid spread of HIV and the increased number orphans. The greatest service one can give to households, especially orphans and vulnerable children, is empowerment.

## Concluding with the story of Lazarus

> And at his gate lay a poor man named Lazarus, covered with sores, who longed to satisfy his hunger with what fell from the rich man's table; even the dogs would come and lick his sores (Lk 16:20–21).

While the traditional interpretation of this story usually focuses on charity, on how the poor man should be helped, or on the immorality of denying food to those in need, this story can also be read from the perspective of labor. This man does not and cannot work because of his medical condition. People unable to work as a result of their health suffer material and psychological pressure because of their inability to provide for themselves. As the number of those affected by HIV and AIDS grows, the pressures they have to bear are shared by their communities, especially the caregivers. This has been and continues to be the case in most of Africa. While encouragement must continue to be given to those who have been supporting the sick, new ways must be found to ensure that the workforce, ravaged by the HIV and AIDS pandemic, is given easy access to antiretroviral drugs, and companies that discriminate against HIV positive employees must be legislated against.

# God's Work—Our Hands; Why Aristotle was Wrong

### Roger Schmidt

## Comments of a listener

How do we define "work"? Does listening to various presentations on the relationship between work and theology constitute work even if it is enjoyable and thought provoking to immerse oneself fully in the speakers' perspectives? In the following, I shall give some preliminary reflections on what I heard during the seminar on the "Theology of Labor."

The day-long seminar certainly gave me much to think about and I was especially interested in continuing to reflect on one specific aspect that was touched upon several times, namely the dignity of work. How can we describe the dignity of work in theological terms, and how can the church contribute to people realizing that dignity?

As we heard several times: the basis of the dignity of work is the conviction that God is a worker. According to the first creation story, God worked in creating the world and had to rest on the seventh day. This means that God did not just work once at the beginning of time. The doctrine of the *creatio continua* makes clear that the work of creation continues. Whatever is in this universe depends on God's continuing work. This is directly connected to the Lutheran understanding of grace when it is related to the First Article of the Apostles' Creed; in and for everything we depend on God.

While the concept of work gains dignity in knowing that God is a worker, does that then actually apply to human work? If we depend on God's work in everything, does our work have any merit? Or, as the second creation story in Genesis seems to suggest, is it just a consequence of sin (cf. Gen 3:19)? Moreover, some people seem to regard work as a punishment rather than a dignified activity. Classical philosophical tradition distinguishes between different types of work. Thus, remunerated work only existed to sustain oneself and thus may appear like a punishment while the leisurely activities of art and philosophy were regarded as ethically far superior forms of work.

This idea was not only prevalent among the philosophers. Christian theologians also have to take care not to create a similar impression. Would it not be according to our true human nature wholly to depend on God's work rather than on our own? Does not trusting one's own work but only God's show faith in its fullness? Would that not be paradise? Therefore, one might continue to ask, Is work at best a necessity under the conditions of the fallen world? Or could it be even worse? Could work simply be the consequence of our disbelief and our inability fully to trust in God's mercy? We find this reasoning among the great ascetics of the Christian and other traditions.

I do not take this suggestion lightly. There is a real possibility that God's work delegitimizes our human work. Especially Reformed anthropology has a clear understanding of the purpose of human existence. And this purpose is definitely not work. The "real work" of the believer lies in praising God in worship. Without a doubt, this is a correct interpretation of the rediscovery of God's grace during the Reformation. The deeper meaning is the believer's recognition that we fully depend on God and that our work can never redeem us. Saying that the purpose of our existence is worship means exactly this: it puts me in the right place within the wider order of creation, as a recipient of God's grace.

But what does this imply for my work? Is work really futile and not part of my true nature?

The second creation story in Genesis—already cited above as a proponent of a pessimistic view on labor—casts doubt on such a simplistic understanding of work. While Adam clearly is not involved in the creation of the world, he is the one who, in a sense, puts the finishing touches on God's good creation. He gives names to all the animals (Gen 2:20). Pursuing this line of thought has given rise to the concept that, as the image of God, human beings might be cocreators with God. This puts a more positive spin on human work. Clearly the language here is not very precise: Where does the work of the human being begin and where does it end? Where exactly is God's work in the work of human beings.

This question becomes even more pertinent if we believe that we work according to God's mandate. This question could be downplayed in times when the church's primary and virtually sole function was to proclaim the Word of God and to ensure proper Christian education. The work of the church and that of Christians according to their Christian calling could be distinguished from the work of the "world."

However, in the eighteenth century, when churches worldwide began to set up the structures for evangelism and diakonia, this question became increasingly urgent. Here were Christians who did not see their Christian calling as being predominantly in Sunday morning worship. While they worked hard during the week, according to their understanding it was no longer worldly work. Their work followed Christ's mandate, citing for evangelism mainly the

Great Commission (Mt 28:16–20). Diaconal work based itself on Matthew 25:31–46 for example.

Increasingly this understanding challenged the theological system. Is the relationship between God and the church really one of principal and agent? Does God just give a mandate and let people fulfill it? Obviously that cannot be true even though traditional language about mission would seem to indicate precisely this. How can it be expressed differently? This important question was one that twentieth-century mission theologians dealt with seriously. Mission was no longer something that could be reduced to a specific activity, and clearly not something that individuals do. Mission became the term for the church's entire outreach. And even that does not describe mission fully. Mission is not a principal—agent relationship between God and church. The Triune God is both: principal and agent. God sends Godself in Jesus Christ and the spirit in order to do the work of mission in proclaiming the good news, caring for the needy, and speaking out for those who are treated unjustly. The church does not own mission; it merely participates in it. In short, the Evangelical Lutheran Church in America (ELCA) expresses this theological conviction as follows: "God's work—Our hands."

While this definition does not solve the problem regarding the distinction between God's work and that of human beings, I nonetheless believe this to be a good working formulation when it comes to the church's work, even if it does not fully clarify the relationship between the work of an individual and that of God.

In order to do so, we will need to reconnect with Luther's understanding of vocation. Luther definitely believed the worship of God to be the very core of the Christian vocation. When it comes to salvation, the core of Luther's understanding of the gospel is to accept that God in Jesus Christ has done all the work. Throughout his life, Luther stressed that human beings cannot contribute to their salvation; they are mere recipients. Whereas it would have been easy to emphasize God's work so strongly that there would be no room left for human work, Luther managed not to let this understanding slip into advocating for a contemplative lifestyle as the sole expression of faith. On the contrary, even everyday tasks such as cleaning a house gain dignity by being understood as being a vocation ordained by God. Probably, this understanding is even easier for Luther because there is no doubt that cleaning the house is not connected to one's salvation.

Luther theology of vocation speaks powerfully about the dignity of work. My work, as mundane as it may seem, is actually worship because I regard it as worship—in faith. The idea that work is dignified in and by itself and not through outside validation is countercultural in many contexts. Asked about his recruitment policy, Mark Zuckerberg, the founder and current CEO of

Facebook responded, "Someone who is exceptional in their role is not just a little better than somebody who is pretty good. They are a hundred times better."[1]

To judge the dignity of work in terms of the product and not from the perspective of the one working is certainly not a new problem. Aristotle made a classic distinction between two types of work. The first type of work creates something new. This applies to the potter, the baker, the carpenter, the artist and the philosopher. The other type of work maintains that which has already been created. That is something the cleaner or the nurse does. Not surprisingly then that Aristotle had a rather elitist preference for the creative aspects of work and his approach finds a wide following even today. Somebody who creates is more admired than somebody who maintains—however ably. And this opens up the possibility to judge the worker in terms of the product—as Zuckerberg does.

Looking simply at the product does not ensure the dignity of work. We have to follow Luther's lead and have a closer look at the process of work. Several thinkers have been reflecting on the changing meaning of work in our postindustrial society. Critiquing the old patterns, Seth Godin, for example, provides resources for an understanding of work as cocreation.[2] It is no longer true that, as Woody Allen once said, eighty percent of success is just showing up. That might have been the case in the industrial era, when humans basically acted as extensions to machines. When machines set the pace and the rhythm, then simply showing up was enough to earn a living. However, in the Western postindustrial societies, as well as in many others, this is no longer holds true. Machines do not need extensions; they are increasingly able to do what they are designed to do without the help of human beings. Human work, therefore, has to be categorically different from that of machines. This not only applies to the artist or the computer programmer, but also to the Starbucks barista and the nightly cleaning brigade. According to Godin, the difference is the human capacity for creating. When humans work, they are able to understand that they are working for other people. Their creation might not consist of a tangible and lasting product, but they can create a meaningful interaction.

For me, this is a secular reading of Luther's theology of vocation. Work is dignified not by its product but by the mindset (or faith) of the one performing it. Work is worship by serving God and the neighbor, and human work receives its dignity through the connection to the source of everything: God, the worker.

---

[1] Cited in *New York Times*, 18 May 2011, at **www.nytimes.com/2011/05/18/technology/18talent.html**.

[2] Cf. Seth Godin, *Linchpin* (London: Hachette, 2010).